THROW Me THE ROPE

A Memoir on Loving Lauren

A Young Woman's Sober Journey to the Human Spirit

LYNDA ZUSSMAN

ABOUT THE AUTHOR

Lynda Zussman, teacher, educator and writer, wrote two screenplays in the 90's, Panic and Papa Rose. As a Special Education educator to children and young adults, she guided others by studying and developing her own spirituality. Nothing prepared her for the death of her 26-year-old daughter, but by writing Throw Me the Rope she has embraced courage, hope, and faith through her daughter's life lessons and spiritual growth. Zussman lives in Newport Beach, California with her husband and dogs, Lexi and Cowboy.

Throw Me the Rope

A Memoir on Loving Lauren

For David and Ashlie: To Life
And to All of Lauren's Angels

THROW ME THE ROPE

One morning, a five year old girl came to her mother, complaining of a recurring, disturbing dream. With a sweet, innocent voice she described to her mother the dream in which she was sinking in quicksand. The mother, with a soothing voice, told her daughter to imagine mommy "throwing her a rope."

A few days later, the excited girl came to her mother to report that the rope had saved her, and the dream was no longer a concern.

Well Lauren, with your passing, I now need you to...

"Throw Me the Rope"

CONTENTS

PROLOGUE

It is Monday morning, Memorial Day 2008, at 8:45 in Newport Beach, California. The dreaded phone call that no parent should ever get comes. It is our wedding anniversary this bright and cheerful day. My husband and I just counted our blessings at a romantic Italian restaurant the night before. We met and married within a month, Memorial Day 1978, exactly thirty years ago. There is much to celebrate. We have two loving daughters. We have our health, our careers, our friends and our family unit. We live in beautiful Southern California, near the Pacific Ocean. These are to be our best years, and yet one phone call changes our lives forever.

CHAPTER I

The Day the Earth Stood Still - A Fallen Angel

"If something comes to life in others because of you, then you have made an approach to immortality."

Norman Cousins

It is Memorial Day, May 26, 2008. On a beautiful sunny day in New York's Central Park, Lauren Nicole Zussman, age 26, decides to go for a short jog with her beloved, Alex. They have been dating for eight months and plan to make a life together. The day has been blissful for them as they continue to enjoy a romantic weekend.

Suddenly, Lauren collapses for no apparent reason. With Alex at her side, a retired policeman calls for help as a crowd surrounds the tragic event. Within minutes, three doctors come to Lauren's rescue as they, too, are enjoying the day at the park. CPR begins immediately and the retired policeman calls an ambulance. Alex holds Lauren's feet up to circulate blood back to her heart. Everyone is participating, but very little sign of life, if any, is present. Fifteen minutes later, the ambulance appears. Defibrillators and additional interventions are used over and over again. Lauren is rushed to Lennox Hill Hospital where a team of doctors and nurses work endlessly for close to an hour. Every emergency procedure fails to sustain any life. An hour and a half after Lauren hit the ground, she is pronounced dead. This is the story of a fallen angel.

The phone rings and an unfamiliar male voice ask if I am the mother of a Lauren Zussman who lives in Manhattan. My mouth goes dry and I hear myself say, "Yes, yes, what's wrong?" In an authoritative voice, he identifies himself as a New York policeman and tells me to call The Lennox Hills Hospital.

"Is she okay?" I ask. He tells me they are working on her and he gives me the number to call. Adrenaline kicks in as I jot down the phone number, along with Alex's number, and scream downstairs to my husband that Lauren is in trouble. I have jelly legs as I walk to the top of the stairs and freeze in the hallway. It is David who calls the hospital.

Lauren is very healthy, or so we thought. She has had many trips to the hospital for a pine nut allergy in the past. During an attack, the throat can close up and one can go into anaphylactic shock. Although life threatening, I have a feeling that this is unrelated and much more serious.

David immediately reaches the ER doctor and I hold my breath, praying to God that she is okay. I picture her licking a Popsicle, recovering from a benign problem. Perhaps it is an asthma attack, although she has not had one in years. Perhaps it is heat stroke. As he listens intently to the details, David's face turns white and then gray. Finally, he says, "Is my daughter okay?" Then he repeats the doctor's words. "She's dead!" I hear a woman screaming out of control. I am this woman. My husband ends the call and tries to calm me down, but to no avail. I am entering into a room of Hell–a room that no parent should enter.

David is in shock, colorless, white-lipped. We know we have to get Ashlie over to the house immediately to tell her about her sister.

Because it is Memorial Day, she is not at work and David reaches her right away. He tells Ashlie that her sister is in the hospital and she needs to come to the house. She hears me scream in the background, and I think she knows what is coming. When she arrives within minutes, we tell her the news in a whisper. We all cry and we are in shock. I don't know what to do. Who do we call? We are all frozen in time as the three of us huddle together. Who do we call? We make a couple of phone calls. Within minutes our neighbors and close friends scurry over, and begin to make phone calls for us. Soon our rescue team fills the dark house of despair.

My husband receives an immediate phone call about donating Lauren's organs, and he agrees on the spot. Lauren would have wanted to be a donor. She was constantly being of service to others, while she was here on earth. Perhaps her eyes would help someone to see. Perhaps her other organs could save a life.

Three Newport Beach policemen appear at our door to check on us. They were notified by the New York police. When the New York policeman called me, he knew that Lauren was gone, but apparently he wanted us to hear it from the doctor. One officer leads me out to the front of our house for air. He has red hair and freckles and is young enough to be my son. I am numb and in shock. We sit on a bench under the tree as I babble. I have no idea what I am saying. I take his hand, only to feel life, as I feel myself leave my body. I only want to wake up from this nightmare. This has to be a damn nightmare. I pinch my skin, and I start to realize that this is no dream. I am going out of my mind. I am going to explode into a million pieces. I start to rock and sit in silence. Finally, I go back into the house and check on my family. We thank the policemen and they leave with sympathetic faces. I then go upstairs to call Alex.

We speak with poor Alex by phone, as he is still at the hospital. His gentle, quiet voice tells me he does not know what happened, and I know he is in shock. His father and a social worker are at his side. He keeps repeating that he does not know what happened, and then he says "We were so happy." His father is a minister and, along with his good friend Mike, calms Alex down as reality starts to penetrate.

Our Rabbi, Mark M. Miller, comes over immediately. I am sure he is used to seeing families in this crippling condition; however, I wonder how many times he sees a young woman leave this earth. I ask the Rabbi, "How could God do this?" and he responds with authority, "God did not do this."

I can't comprehend the meaning of this tragedy. How could this possibly happen? I think human nature keeps the mind from fully processing this reality. Every time I get close to the truth, I wobble with weak knees, yet an adrenaline rush shocks my system. I cry intermittently while I speak to my friends and family. It is painful to watch my husband go through this; I honestly do not think he will make it through the day.

Ash is in shock, but holds up pretty well. We keep close and hug throughout the day. I hear chatter among the bodies that surround us as I drift in and out. My feet are not on the ground and my comprehension is limited. The clock is no longer ticking. We are all in a state of denial and on another plane. This indescribable state of being has never before been experienced by our family. Suddenly, there is no past, no future. There is only unfathomable pain and numbness. We are crushed.

Later in the day a funeral director, recommended by our Rabbi, comes over and takes care of all the details, including flying Lauren home from New York. I don't think my husband and I could have sustained a trip to New York in our condition, when we can barely stand up. The darkness surrounding David is in stark contrast to our all-white kitchen. He continues to sob and I worry about him the most.

Ash is still holding up as well as she can. I know I have to be strong for David and for Ash, even though I am in Hell. There is no other way to describe this state of terror. How can a healthy, beautiful woman fall to her death while jogging for eight minutes? Of what health problem were we not aware? Why would this happen to her?

Lauren had a healthy heart but according to her autopsy, she died from cardiovascular disease. They label this a natural death, but to us it was anything but natural. She was at a normal weight and ate mostly a vegetarian diet with tons of salmon. How could this happen? The report cites that an arrhythmia, along with blockage of her thin

4

coronary arteries, caused her to go into cardiac arrest while jogging. Was it the perfect storm, or was it simply her time? Were the planets lined up just so? Six weeks prior to this event we had seen a healthy, vibrant young woman who lit up a room with her smile. The calling of her life has come without an invitation. The fierce interruption strips us of our tomorrows, our dreams, our visions of what could be. The logic of physics, of nature, of the higher power, fades along with the abstract medical information. The answers are vague, with weak supporting evidence that anything had been wrong.

An energy force no longer exists as we face the darkness of Lauren's death. It is surreal. It is blunt. It is heartless. As time goes by, how am I to turn weakness into strength during this dreadful time? How do I stand up to the plate, when my ankles are tied with unbearable, profound grief? I just have to do it.

Lauren had overcome exceptional challenges, and had succeeded beautifully in having a very fulfilling life over the last eight years. She was at the top of her game. Her career with the Ford Modeling Agency and her personal love life with Alex were soaring. After conquering her demons of depression and alcoholism, she only wanted to be of service to others. As Freud said, "Work and Love are all that really matters."

She had it all–beauty, intelligence, compassion, courage, generosity, integrity, love, and family–and yet, it was taken away within minutes. She was an angel and the other angels were calling her name.

The Daily Pilot of Newport Beach, a division of The Los Angeles Times, published the following story on Lauren the day after her passing. The writer, Daniel Telford, knew me from an article that he wrote on my high school special education English class which was published by the Times. After learning of Lauren's death, he wanted to write an article about her amazing life.

Model 'was always focusing on the light'

Family and coworkers remember former OCC student as an inspiring person who turned her life around. She was 26.

By Daniel Tedford
Daily Pilot

Eight years ago, Lauren Nicole Zussman was on a path to destruction.

She'd had success as a model, but she was an alcoholic and had just finished a binge while on a Memorial Day vacation at Lake Havasu. She ended up in the hospital, near death.

Days later, she walked into a local bank and told her story to an OCC counselor who worked at the bank.

"I want you in my office at 4 p.m. tomorrow," Zussman's mother Lynda recalled the counselor telling Lauren.

Zussman, who died unexpectedly Monday, turned her life around after that meeting with the counselor. She dedicated the last eight years of her life to telling her story to youths so they would avoid the same troubles.

Zussman, 26, died of apparent heart failure while jogging through New York's Central Park.

"She was always focusing on the light instead of the darkness," Lynda Zussman said. "And she brought that to the people she helped."

Zussman was mostly known within the modeling world as a designer fit model, working for various agencies and modeling clothes for designers Thakoon, Proenza Schouler and Jill Stuart, said Ford Models Inc. Vice President Wendy Ford.

"She was very professional with a lot of technical experience, which made her a desired fit model in the business," Ford said. "She was an awesome model and got to where she was meant to be and did her job really well."

Zussman worked closely with designers, trying on clothes before they went to the runways to make sure they fit and looked perfect.

Proenza Schouler said she was just the model they needed when they were trying to get their designs ready.

"With Lauren's contribution, we would turn our design ideas over to the big world," Proenza Schouler designer Weronika Olbrychska said. "We miss the time we have spent with Lauren and feel grateful to have gotten to know her in her bright, if all too short, life."

But it was her work outside modeling for which friends and family will remember her most.

"She didn't want her beauty to be a distraction," said Lynda Zussman, who is a teacher at Newport Harbor High School. "God gave her a second chance, and she found herself. Her death wasn't in vain."

Zussman graduated from her Calabasas high school early and attended OCC at 16. Zussman's parents remember their daughter prior to her near-death experience as often nervous and angry.

Their relationship was strained, and they worried about their daughter.

But Lauren turned herself around after she got help. Compassion became her first priority, and her relationship with her parents began to flourish.

"She was eight years' sober when she died.

"She had a lot of tumbles," Zussman said of her daughter. "But when she was down and out, all she had to do was help a girl."

She attended Alcoholics Anonymous meetings regularly. When she was younger, she would fly to New York to work as model, but would always return to Costa Mesa to attend meetings and speak to struggling local youths. She spoke at Costa Mesa High School in 2001, and was doing a lot of public speaking during the last five years while she lived in Manhattan.

She had started at New York University to get her degree in life coaching more than a year ago.

"She was a real natural at modeling," Lynda Zussman said. "She loved the fashion and posing, but it wasn't fulfilling."

What Zussman did find satisfying was her work with others. She would often sponsor four people at AA at one time, helping them on weekends with their 12 steps.

Her mother remembers her Thanksgiving visit and spending half her time helping shelters or others in need.

"She knew she had a higher calling," Lynda said. "She gave her strength. Her biggest lesson in life was to use your muscle — self-determination."

"I loved my daughter very much," her father, David Zussman, said.

BEAUTY: Lauren Nicole Zussman, a model, died Monday.

Lauren Nicole Zussman is survived by her father, David; mother, Lynda; sister, Ashlie; her fiance, Alex Scott; aunts Judy Ticktin, Pat Brown and Tami Zussman; and uncles Harold Ticktin, Roger Brown and Marc Zussman. Services will be at the Hillside Memorial in Los Angeles on Friday.

In lieu of flowers, the family is asking for gifts to be donated to the Orangewood Children's Foundation at 1575 E. 17th St., Santa Ana, (714) 619-0200.

DANIEL TEDFORD may be reached at (714) 966-4632 or at daniel.tedford@latimes.com.

During the week following Lauren's death, endless phone calls, flowers, cards and platters of food arrive at our house. The people at our local high school where I work call and they are in shock, as many had met Lauren. Our good friends are at our sides and many stay for hours. Neighbors and friends continue to give their support and condolences. Close friends from Los Angeles drive down immediately to be with us. David's business partner and his cousin appear at our door with comforting arms. It's amazing how everyone drops everything to help us walk through this nightmare. Through their tears, they give us the comfort we need. Lauren touched us all, and our friends and family help us get through the next few days. Funeral arrangements are being made as David and I try to rest.

My husband and I cannot eat or sleep. I only drink water and later in the week I eat a little bit of yogurt. I proceed to move with nervous energy as my husband continuously sobs. The people around me think I am so strong, but in reality, I am barely functioning. Our doctor stops by and prescribes medication so that we can at least sleep. At the beginning, it has no effect, but later we manage to have some sleep.

The funeral is now planned for Friday, 5-30-08…five plus three is eight. The mysterious number keeps appearing. Lauren passed on 5-26-08…two plus six is eight. The year is 2008. Lauren had been sober for eight years; she passed away unexpectedly eight years from the day she almost died overdosing on alcohol in 2000. Lauren always had an infatuation with the number 8 because it represented infinity. We have the funeral director walk us through all the steps prior to the funeral. David and I are sobbing across the dining table as she helps us pick a coffin. Later in the week, our Rabbi comes over the day before the funeral and he interviews David and me. We speak about the many wonderful traits that define our Lauren: thoughtful, kind, inspirational. We sit in our backyard and I feel this surreal experience, almost like I am watching a scene from a movie. From the outside I am looking in. Why are there so many people in my house serving food? Why are flowers showing up at the door? Why is my husband crying in between each sentence?

The Rabbi remembers meeting Lauren privately a few years ago, discussing the enlightenment of sobriety, and how helping others was her calling in life. He has an easy time painting the canvas to prepare his eulogy on Lauren. This is a tribute to a young, beautiful, woman who overcame her demons and inspired others to be their best. Lauren's brave journey was shortened, for reasons we will never understand while we are here on earth. I write the funeral announcement for the newspaper. That too, is easy, as the pen begins to flow.

Lauren Nicole Zussman, age 26, our beautiful daughter (sister) died suddenly while jogging in Central Park in New York. Lauren moved to New York 5 1/2 years ago and was a Ford International Model. Lauren was attending NYU to become a life coach and her passion was to help young people live their best lives. Eight years sober, Lauren was constantly of service to others and was loved by many on both coasts. Born and raised in Southern California, her heart was with the sun and water. Lauren's healthy, holistic life included yoga, nutrition, cooking, painting, writing and mastering Italian. Lauren was a joyous shining star who regularly spoke at AA meetings and high schools and worked with disadvantaged young women. Her spirit will live on forever in all of our hearts. She met and fell in love with her beloved, Alex Scott. In lieu of flowers, kindly make donations in memory of Lauren to Orangewood Children's Foundation, Santa Ana, CA.

I receive a box from Alex before the funeral that has Lauren's phonebook in it. I make the dreaded calls to tell her Los Angeles friends and co-workers of her passing. Each phone call is harder than the next, and although I could have delegated this chore to others, I felt responsible to call these people. I have to call one of Lauren's best friends, Jessie. The two "fairy sisters" met when they were 16 and had many adventures while Lauren lived in California. Amanda and Lindsay, Lauren's childhood friends, break down as I relate the devastating news. The girls read beautiful eulogies at the funeral, recalling the endless memories of growing up together.

David calls The Ford Modeling Agency in New York to deliver the shocking news. Later, a New York Memorial would be planned for the many friends and clients that could not attend the L.A. funeral.

8

Lauren is to be prepared for her last viewing, and we all gather the night before to attend the most bittersweet day of our lives. Eulogies are prepared, relatives and friends arrive at the airport, and last details are assembled, as we all take the steps to honor our daughter's life.

∽

CHAPTER 2

Baby Lauren: A Dream Comes True

"Truth is a deep kindness that teaches us to be content in our everyday life and share with the people the same happiness."

Kahlil Gibran

After being married for a couple of years, David and I try to get pregnant. Month after month, nothing happens. Over a year goes by and I start to become concerned.

Then, on a trip to Las Vegas in November of 1980, we survived the terrible, infamous MGM Grand fire. David and I are rescued on the seventeenth floor, hours after the fire breaks out. Eighty-five people had died, many from our floor. We are hospitalized for two days because of smoke inhalation. We are damn lucky to have survived this fire. The inferno makes national news and because of this fire, water sprinklers are now mandatory, as they were absent in The MGM. We decide now to really try and have this baby.

It is time for fertility treatments so we consult with Dr. Ed Stadler, a well-known infertility specialist, who has auburn hair and a calm bedside manner. He tells me with confidence that he will get me pregnant; that is, he will help us get pregnant. However, fertility tests are not fun. I nervously drive to the doctor's office for the results, as I prepare my speech for David, thinking it is his fault. "Sweetie, we could always adopt and I love you very much"–that sort of thing. Sitting in front of our doctor, we hear that David's sperm is in the sperm donor category. The two men grin at each other, like it is a boy's club and I am not invited. I swear that after that statement, David kicks the door open with his cowboy boot, raring to go. Nothing makes a man feel better than to hear that he has potent sperm.

So the focus is now on me and I go for test after test. It is established that at the peak time of conception, my hormones are weak, so I take Clomid, a mild fertility drug. I am now taking my temperature to time my ovulation and chart it, like a good scientist. With Dr. Stadler's magic potion of hormones, I soon become pregnant, even though I am still stressed from the fire. I lose the baby a few weeks later. It is the beginning of experiencing true loss. We try again a couple of months later and our Lauren is happily conceived. The whole process takes many months, but at thirty, I am going to have our baby!

I throw up every day adjusting to the hormone changes, but I feel pretty good. Every morning, I go to Bob's Big Boy and order everything on the menu. I am ravenous so I eat pancakes, eggs, bacon, potatoes, orange juice, and milk.

David and I take Lamaze classes, but it turns out Lauren wants to do this her own way and I end up having a caesarian section. My water breaks a month early and I arrive at the hospital Sunday morning. Eight hours later at 4:44 PM, a star is born.

Lauren is a good-natured baby, but she does not take to breast feeding. She wants the bottle and only the bottle. After many unsuccessful attempts, our pediatrician convinces us to put her on the bottle. Tearfully I do, but I feel like a failure. I have to get over it and move on because she is starving after one week. The doctor tells me that premature babies sometimes have trouble sucking, so I decide I would hold her very close to me and bond with her. I cry all the way home with raging hormones.

When Lauren is eight months old, my husband decides to leave his position at a Newport Beach law firm and start a financial television program. The start-up business produces no income and there is a lot of stress. We have a new baby, a new house, a new mortgage, and no monthly income other than a small savings. I develop a thyroid problem, commonly known to develop post-pregnancy. My body is pushed to the max and I develop terrible panic attacks during this time. My mom visits from Chicago for a few weeks to help and David is very involved with the care of the baby. Between the two of them, we all manage, but for a while there is a separation between mommy and baby. I feel like a zombie and I am flat. I struggle daily and cannot help the state of my body nor my mind. I feel guilty and this makes me feel worse. For the first time in my life, I experience clinical depression and I am often anxious. I see a doctor for the symptoms and cry a lot.

Four months later, with the help of medication, I become the doting mother I was meant to be. Years later, while watching our family videos, I observe a healthy interaction between Lauren and me. My mom takes Lauren for walks in the stroller and she notices her silently gazing at the flowers with an incredible intensity. She thinks that this is unusual and calls her an "old soul." At one time my Mom asks if it is normal for a baby to be so calm–no crying, no fussing. I think I am lucky, as we see other babies carry on.

Lauren's first birthday is a huge celebration with a typical overdone party. We are once again a happy threesome, caring for this beautiful baby. At this time, Lauren never crawls and we are a little concerned. Then something miraculous happens. David and I are watching TV, with Lauren at our side. She is playing with one of her toys, wearing a sweet, floral dress. In a split minute, we see her climb up on the edge of our paisley couch. She looks like a proud rooster and takes off. Our jaws drop and we can't believe our eyes, but that is just Lauren. When she puts her mind to something, she can achieve it.

Months later David's T.V. show, *Financial Inquiry*, expands and becomes extremely successful. We decide to sell our house in Irvine and move back to Los Angeles when Lauren is 18 months old.

I am thrilled to return to the city. I first met David in L.A., while I was teaching school. Although Orange County is lovely with nature and the Pacific Ocean, it is very underdeveloped at this time. Our friends and relatives will now live near us and it is a new energy to embrace.

Lauren's early days start in Los Angeles, California. We buy a house off of Mulholland Drive and Beverly Glen. Our new home is on the outskirts of the Bel Air mansions. We have a small, quaint shopping center a couple of blocks away, where every celebrity dines or shops. The center is a great place to hang out for coffee, snacks, and lunch. The rows of stores, with a great little deli, are nested in a cul-de-sac.

My days are often spent at the famous Stephen S. Wise Temple, attending "Mommy and Me" classes or going on play dates at the park. We are fortunate to have a live-in housekeeper, Moray, a lovely Filipino, middle-aged, soft-spoken woman who becomes part of our family. Moray has no children of her own but clearly she is a good role model. Upon their meeting for the first time, Moray asks Lauren her name. Lauren peeks out of her room and says, "My name is Punky Brewster." Punky Brewster is the popular T.V. show personality that Lauren watches regularly. Moray actually believes her, until I come around the corner to make the formal introduction.

At two and a half, Lauren's sister Ashlie arrives, and although not completely thrilled, Lauren welcomes her little sister. Ash is an easy baby and oddly enough, her conception happens immediately with no drugs or temperature charts. Moray and Lauren pair up immediately, as I am with Ashlie around the clock. Ash takes very well to breastfeeding and we are joined at the hip. Lauren becomes more aware of the new baby and is a bit jealous. Most of this is normal when a new baby enters the family unit, but I think Lauren had an unusual attachment to David and me; therefore, it was even harder for her.

Although we try to make a smooth transition, Lauren starts to have reservations about the new arrival. She often seems lost and confused around the baby and is not quite sure what to make of it. We buy a stuffed black and white pony, ring the doorbell, and try to convince Lauren that Ash sent the pony. It works for a while; however, when you're used to being the center of attention, particularly with Mom and Dad, a new sibling changes the dynamics of the family.

Lauren cooks and cleans with Moray and they have fun making sandwiches for their picnics, baking chocolate chip cookies or cooking rice and fish. Moray introduces Lauren to some of her homeland foods.

But having two babies, two and a half years apart, is like having twenty. Sometimes it is overwhelming. I realize that I did not put soap in the washing machine. Yesterday's meal is still in the microwave. I see other calm mothers at the grocery store, with four kids in their cart, pointing out the difference between an orange and a grapefruit. On the other hand, I grab what I need and leave quickly and sometimes I am befuddled. Even reading the newspaper is out of the question. It is a job that never quits, but this is what all mothers do.

I have another series of panic attacks, again post-pregnancy, but they are quickly under control and short-lived with the proper medication and therapy. Here we go again. Having any kind of mental distress is not openly discussed or written about back in the '80s. I quietly learn to live with the anxiety of having anxiety, and in spite of it, mingle well with my neighbors and friends.

I am now going to four "Mommy and Me" classes, two a week for each daughter. The wheels on the bus go round and round and round and round, four times, but I make some good friendships, and we are all the thirty-something generation, living in the moment.

On family outings, we see other children fuss in restaurants, while Lauren asks us to pass the sugar. I am a little concerned that she doesn't cry or fuss. I observe the normal developments in Ashlie, however; she too is a peach, but with more animation and expressions. Ash plays more and connects to her peers. Lauren often prefers to play alone and does not want to join the others.

On Sunday nights, Lauren and I go for sushi at our local Center, and she flirts with the sushi chefs. They flirt back with a slick smile and a wink of the eye. It is our weekly ritual. Eating sushi together continues to be one of our simple pleasures throughout the years.

Moray often takes the girls up to the center during the afternoon. It is a safe haven in the neighborhood. She enjoys her time with our children. Sometimes there is a discipline problem, and I have to intervene. Occasionally, Moray says in broken English, "Mrs. Zussman, Lauren hit Ashlie." I have that little talk with Lauren about keeping her hands to herself, and she rolls her eyes, as if I told her she has to eat her broccoli.

Meanwhile, David continues to focus on expanding his financial television show, but always plays with each daughter, especially on the weekends. The gang goes to the local amusement parks, visits David's parents, or drives to the golden arches. Lauren, knowing the routine, announces with excitement, "Look, the golden arches, the golden arches!"

We are a close-knit family with good friends. It seems like we are always celebrating holidays and birthdays, with delicious food being a main attraction. I love cookbooks and new recipes and manage to take some cooking lessons at a local high school. We are all foodies. We have a small pool/spa in the backyard and a community pool in the neighborhood. The girls practically live in the water during the summer. When we are at Mommy and Me, I notice that Lauren does not like to sit on my lap very often, like the rest of the Moms with their babies. She prefers to walk around and study the bulletin boards. The colorful pictures interest her more than joining the group.

At age four, Lauren attends an interview at a prominent Bel-Air private school. The headmaster, with piercing, slate eyes, and thin, pasty, magenta lips, begins the questioning. In her condescending manner, she quizzes Lauren with the necessary annoying questions: "Where do you go to school now?" "How old are you?" The headmaster's breath smells like Listerine, possibly a decoy for a former alcoholic indulgence. Finally she asks Lauren what her name is, as Lauren does not make eye contact, and is disinterested. Lauren, with an authoritative voice, says, "My name is Queen Esther and I can rule the world." She has just gone to a Purim Carnival at preschool. The frumpy, white-haired woman purses her wrinkled lips and does not like Lauren's fantasy world of the Old Testament. Needless to say, my daughter is not asked to join this prestigious school. She always had the talent of re-inventing herself, and if Lauren did not like you, she would disappear into her bubble of make-believe.

Soon after, Lauren enters a Montessori preschool. We attend a few interviews and hope to be accepted. Celebrity children attend this Bel-Air school and it has an excellent reputation. Being a former classroom teacher, I think this progressive form of education will be best for Lauren, especially since she has not been very stimulated by last year's nursery school. She has advanced language, has an intense interest in books, and loves to draw. Our friends can't believe her early language and she seems more like a midget than a small child. My neighbor takes Lauren to McDonald's with her daughter, and the woman tells me that Lauren read the back of the Happy Meal. I do not know how or where she learned this.

Lauren often inquires about Ashlie and me. "Mommy, what do you and Ashlie do when I am at school?" she asks with a raised eyebrow. Lauren is excited to go to school but just as excited to come home. However, during the ages from four to six, we observe some aggressive behavior while Lauren is playing with the neighborhood children. The horrible fours are setting in to make up for the lack of the terrible twos.

Lauren receives a negative report from her Montessori teacher. The teacher observes signs of defiant behavior during the second year in preschool. Lauren does not want to participate with the other children. She often refuses to sit with the children or she wanders back into the empty classroom during recess. Lauren pulls all the napkins out of the box in the bathroom, and throws them all over the place. This turns into a school visit for Mom and Dad.

David was a typical hyperactive child, so we check it off as a chip off the old block. Lauren's behavior becomes an issue, yet we had to just about stand on our heads to get her into this school. The tuition is also expensive, but the reputation of this school is excellent. I think yanking her out of the program at this time will make her feel like a failure.

At the meeting, Miss Susan smiles in a condescending way and ignores my status as a former educator, only to tell me that this is not acceptable behavior. "Miss Susan, can't we work with Lauren's social issues and praise her for positive behavior?"

Miss Susan replies, "Mrs. Zussman, your daughter needs to reform and join the others when I tell her to. She does not participate with the other children and at times she defies me."

"We will speak to her about this." David says.

We both walk away disappointed with the report. I decide to give more one-on-one time to Lauren and play board games with her. I do not understand what she is not getting from us for her to be acting out. My guilt starts to set in.

I consult a child psychologist, Dr. Wendy Mogel, who went on to write a fabulous book, *The Blessing of a Skinned Knee*. Had I read this newly written book when this was all happening, I would have had a different attitude about the whole experience. Lauren is tested, only to find out that she is highly intelligent, that she prefers people to objects (this is why she doesn't want to play with toys), and she wants the adult attention from her parents. Wendy Mogel's concepts are right on. Take the child as is, and don't make them fit into the box. We are trying to have Lauren fit into a circle, when she is clearly a square peg. Even though the school is very progressive, with many stimulating educational concepts, it is not for Lauren.

Life takes a dramatic turn when David is diagnosed with melanoma skin cancer, a life-threatening disease. After discovering a black spot on his back, a biopsy confirms the cancer. A small part of his back is surgically removed, and we are thrilled to find out that it is stage 1 cancer with a 95% cure rate. I bathe the three-inch open wound with hydrogen peroxide, as David cries from the pain. I cry with him. While we did have a five year watch and consult with his oncologist, David decides to have some therapy regarding this life-changing experience. Although he is an attentive father and husband before this event, I see a much more compassionate and appreciative man evolve. He adores his family even more, and stops to smell the roses. It is no longer about making money. Humility and an appreciation for life overcome his sense of being.

Since Lauren is only four at this time, we do not know if this dilemma is affecting her behavior at preschool. We hire another therapist and she sees Dr. Gary, weekly, for the next several months.

While waiting for Dr. Gary to come out to his waiting room, Lauren is patiently sitting with me, reading some magazines. Soon the therapist comes out to call Lauren into his office. Lauren quickly hides under his chairs, as it becomes apparent to her that she will be talking about her feelings. Even at this early age, she is very guarded with her feelings. Not only does Dr. Gary softly coax her into his office, but she really takes a liking to this six-foot-four, slightly bald-headed man. His kind demeanor is clearly a magnet for children and I am pleased. I feel like this is a good fit.

By the age of six, we see a remarkable difference in her interaction with her teachers and her peers. She mainstreams in all areas, educationally and emotionally. I think, through play therapy with Dr. Gary, she makes peace with the emotional conflict that she is experiencing. However, life is like an onion. There are many layers of development through our lifetime and many chapters to experience.

Life is good. I love my modest house that I decorate with bleached-out cabinets, white tile floors and beige Berber carpeting. We put in a little spa-pool in the yard, with Mexican rust pavers, and it is our oasis. We have barbeques frequently as chef Daddy David takes orders and flips those ribs. Our daughters are thriving. Lauren continues to prefer adult company to her peers, but we often have many friends and kiddies at our house. Birthdays, play dates, and social dinners with friends consume us. I have no idea what is going on in the news, and I do not have time to read one book, something that I love to do.

David's business is soaring. He loves creating financial television and coming home to his family. Yes, we are truly happy, and our routine of family life is busy, yet enjoyable. I take a few art classes at UCLA, studying contemporary and modern art and later some screenwriting classes. I write a screenplay on the MGM Hotel fire and sell it as an option.

Moray is right in there with us, as we take many trips together. Hawaii, Las Vegas and local California areas–Palm Springs, La Jolla, and Newport Beach–are places we visit often. We also vacation at The Mandalay Beach Family Resort in Ventura. The girls love to swim all day long, play on the beach, and eat fabulous food. Like many sisters, they are both friend and foe, but often play nicely together. Lauren would still prefer to be the only child, but she finally gets it; it isn't going to happen.

Later, Lauren starts kindergarten at Stephen S. Wise Temple in Bel Air, and does pretty well. There is more integration with her peers, and she becomes an excellent reader. Succeeding at the top of her class improves her self-esteem, and she begins to really like school.

The Hebrew School teacher takes a liking to Lauren and tells her, "You can be the substitute teacher, if I am ever absent." Lauren knows that Mrs. Learner is teasing her, but the positive connection and attention is a plus and Lauren shines. She beams as she tells us the story at the dinner table. Mrs. Learner is a striking, mature brunette who has a true love for children. She was born to be an educator. Her intellect and skills bring the best out of precocious children; thus, the child excels, as did Lauren. God bless, Mrs. Learner.

David and I take a couple of parenting classes, read a lot of books and our lives become more normal with everyday living. However, Lauren's tall body, free spirit and mature mind concern me. She is anything but average, not peculiar, but different than the other children–definitely an "*old soul.*"

When Lauren is six years old we move to Calabasas, an upscale suburb, twenty minutes northwest of Los Angeles. Our Mediterranean, custom home is behind guarded gates and best of all, the public school system is number one in the county. Unlike L.A., our neighborhood is very lively, with all of the kids on the block going to the local school. There are many extra-curricular activities right in our own backyard, and we do not have to spend endless hours in the car.

During Halloween, it looks like a Steven Spielberg movie, with all the kids in their costumes. One would expect ET to be lurking around the corner. My husband and I take turns going door to door trick-or-treating, as this is the most exciting holiday for the kiddies. Joy and excitement is everywhere.

Lauren excels at soccer in second grade, and ends up playing in an All-Star team a few years later. On weekend trips, along with her father, she plays competitive soccer throughout Southern California. This is definitely a self-esteem enhancer as Lauren drags in Sunday night with her father, looking like a beaten warrior. "Mom, we won!" and with that she soundly goes to bed at 6:00 pm with a medal around her neck and a smile on her face. Unfortunately, her active asthma keeps her from continuing. Lauren also attends Hebrew School, Brownies and piano lessons. Friends are always running in and out of our house and our lives ease up. David skis with the girls on weekends and goes to the amusement parks as well.

Lauren still continues to socially integrate with her peers, especially as she becomes older. She makes new friends and becomes more involved with school. In fourth grade, Lauren meets a tall, freckled, red-headed girl down the block. Lindsey and Lauren become fast friends and they bond forever. Lindsey is at my house so often that I adopt her as a third daughter. Her parents like Lauren very much and sleepovers are regular events.

Our house is busy with the girls' friends running in and out. We get a Yorkshire terrier puppy and we name her Muffy, later to be known as Muff Dog. With an adopted cat, Sugar, we are just another suburban family with the normal ups and downs of life. A rabbit and a frog soon join the menagerie.

We are a very close-knit family with a lot of love, laughter and living. For some reason, food is our main attraction and is always on our minds. One time on a family trip, we actually all wake up at 3:00 AM and venture out of our hotel to find a Carl's Junior, only to wolf down giant, greasy burgers and fries. We laugh so hard; we name ourselves "The Rollies." That name sticks with us for many years, even to this day. We were all goofballs that night. All aboard the Cuckoo Train.

Lauren develops a close relationship with her Grandma Janet. Grandma is my mother and she is a sweet, gentle soul who dotes on her granddaughters with unconditional love. If the girls get in trouble at school, it is the fault of the teachers, according to Grandma. A teacher does not let Lauren use the bathroom, and when Lauren tells Grandma, she threatens to bring her boxing gloves to school. She asks if the teacher is mentally ill for denying this request and we all laugh, but that is Grandma, always putting the girls on a pedestal.

Lauren, along with Ash, sees both sets of grandparents on weekends. They are lavished with presents on birthdays and holidays. David's mom, Eleanor, adores the girls in the early years, but comes down with Alzheimer's and it progresses as the girls get older.

It is time to say goodbye to Moray, as the girls are more independent. Moray has an L.A. position waiting for her. We remain friendly, and she often celebrates with the girls at their parties. Little did we know that years later Moray would fly in from Arizona to attend Lauren's funeral.

༒

CHAPTER 3

Family Life: The Good Old Days

"Share light. Expect miracles.
Honor the voice of your inner guide."

Gabrielle Bernstein

It isn't until the seventh grade that we see a change in Lauren's behavior. Remember, there are many layers to an onion. Lauren goes to a sleepover at the house of Sara , who is our neighbor. However, we find out that Lauren and Sara are missing after Sara's father calls us at two in the morning. Immediately, David and I scurry up and down the street in our car looking for the girls. We fear that the girls are kidnapped when the parents find empty beds. Polly Klass, from the Bay area, was kidnapped and murdered at this time, so it makes us all crazy with fear.

Driving around, David and I spot a middle-aged man parked in his black truck. The vehicle has no windows and I am convinced that our girls are in there. I jump out of the car and scream. "Open the doors, open the door, you have my daughter in there!" Although this poor man thinks I am out of my mind at 2:30 in the morning, he agrees to open his empty truck.

A few minutes later we spot Lauren and Sara in the neighborhood, drinking vodka and orange juice, with three neighborhood "bad boys." I start to physically attack these boys for corrupting this poor, innocent child when my husband, the lawyer, holds me back, knowing that a legal battle will follow if I hit them. I am a mother bear protecting my cub. A bad, sneaky cub that also fills our liquor bottles with water after drinking the alcohol with her girlfriends. I retrieve my daughter and think it is time for some therapy.

Things start to settle down and Lauren prepares for her Bat Mitzvah. It is a special time in her life, because it is an accomplishment in Judaism to become a young, responsible woman. After the service, a big party is planned. In lieu of flowers on the tabletops, we opt to make care packages for The Pediatrics Aids Foundation. Along with her friend, Lindsay, we wrap these overflowing care packages in bright, colored, plastic baskets with all kinds of goodies for children until the wee hours into the morning. Lauren enjoys the act of giving and she can't understand why everyone doesn't do this. In this material world, it is a pleasure to witness her enthusiasm, as this is one of her first experiences being of service to others.

Lauren gets excellent grades, but I see a certain amount of rebellious behavior.

Slamming doors and a lot of back talk is tolerated to a certain degree. I think this is part of her adolescence. She is clearly an independent thinker who does not want to conform or necessarily take orders from authority figures. Lauren is assertive, sometimes fearless and feisty with her friends. Although her teachers like her, she will often challenge a grade or homework assignment. If a peer picks on her, she will enter the ring with her boxing gloves.

Life, once again, is pretty normal with doctor's appointments, dentist appointments, school activities, and family outings. It seems like we are over the hurdle, as Lauren seems to be doing well in all areas for years. We think engaging in competitive sports is healthy for her. I think she will choose sports over drugs and alcohol. Unfortunately, it is just a matter of time before Lauren finds both. It is only during her teen-aged years when I discover round two with challenging behavior.

Lauren has a very close relationship with her father, always wanting to be praised for her athletic ability. David always wanted a son and he got the best of both worlds. After her soccer games, David takes Lauren and her friends to McDonald's. They eat endless orders of fries and a couple of burgers. Proudly, she announces that she has "put away power" and she uses that term to amuse us all, even until recently. If it is a Thanksgiving meal, or an elegant restaurant, she has "put away power." Lauren always loves food and is a real foodie.

As with most siblings, Ash and Lauren have a love/hate relationship. If anyone gives Ashlie a hard time on the playground or at school, Lauren will step in and cease the conflict. Girls can be nasty and Ash is a bit passive, but Lauren gets the word out. "You touch my sister and I will beat the shit out of you." Nobody messes with the big sister. The girls have a deep love for each other, and more importantly, they are always there for each other, through thick and thin.

In 1994, we experience the infamous Northridge earthquake. The 6.7 Richter scale tremors traumatize all of us. It is 4:30 in the morning and we honestly do not think we will get out of the house alive, as the roof and house shake uncontrollably. The violent shaker continues as we all run down the stairs. We grab the girls in the hall and run like bats out of hell. Within minutes, our house is in shambles with broken glass everywhere. We all huddle together in the living room, close to the front door, as aftershocks continue. David goes to pick up Grandma Janet the following night and we all slumber in the living room, but we are afraid to go to sleep. It is 3:00 AM in the morning and we are half sleeping. Suddenly, without warning, Lauren runs out into the street, screaming with fear. We go out to settle her down, only to find out later that she has gotten her period for the first time. How traumatic, to experience a natural course of nature in fear, due to an overwhelming disaster. I feel hurt that she does not immediately tell me and chooses to hide it.

We end up having $75,000 in damages. Our house is unlivable. Fortunately, the Ritz Carlton in Marina Del Rey offers to house us at a hundred dollars a night because we are earthquake survivors. As we enter this elegant hotel as wandering gypsies, we are fortunate to be placed on the VIP floor, with complimentary food around the clock. We are on the top floor but we are so delighted with the amenities that we don't care when mild shakers continue. We have two rooms and like living there, even though we have to drive the kids to school 30 miles away. The month-long experience brings us together, during this unstable time, as the workers repair our house.

After this horrendous experience, we decide to buy another house in the neighborhood. Our current house is not on bedrock; another earthquake of a similar magnitude could cause the same damage or worse. We find a new model home that quickly comes on the market with some of its furniture and art. We fall in love with this Mediterranean, turnkey, contemporary home. A flowing fountain spews into a long lap pool. It is slightly smaller than our current house, but it is cozy and safe. The house is priced right and we believe our big house will sell instantly. Wrong. Never own two houses at the same time, thinking that one will sell immediately.

We are stuck with two houses for a couple of years, due to the weak housing market. We rent out the new house, but at a fraction of the mortgage, and we have double taxes to pay. This causes a lot of tension in the house. Lauren is upset with the turmoil, and simultaneously, her grandfather passes away after a long illness. I then come down with a terrible flu that turns into a classic, chronic fatigue syndrome for eighteen months. This impacts Lauren's security at that time. I never knew how this affected her until she told me later in life. Reflecting on that time, we discussed that dark period.

"Mom, I hated that time in my life."

"I know. We had a curse on us."

"I didn't like the constant state of having our house for sale."

"Grandpa was sick for weeks and then died, then I got sick. I know that added to the instability of things."

"I wanted to check out. I wanted to drink."

"You were pretty angry."

"Between the social pressures and coming home to the tension, I wanted to disappear."

"I know honey, I'm sorry. Shit happens, but I *am* sorry."

"It was the beginning of my escape."

"Therapy wasn't enough?"

"No, it wasn't. I felt detached from my body, my mind, my spirit. I didn't want to feel anything. I wanted to be high."

This was a meaningful and profound conversation. Too bad it couldn't have been expressed and dealt with at the time of the events.

Finally, we sell the big house at a major loss, and I recover, but it is a trying time. Lauren attends the same school, has the same friends and even though the new house is a few miles from the old one, she thinks the move is unsettling. Maybe it is.

At 14 years old, Lauren is discovered by an agent from The Ford Modeling Agency. After being told since she was seven years old that she should model, I agree for her to take a workshop. The infamous agent, Nina Blanchard, stops Lauren at the end of the class, and tells her to call Lisa tomorrow at the agency. I am happy and nervous for her at the same time. "Mom, you told me if I get good grades, I could take a crack at modeling." I reluctantly agree.

At this time, she begins modeling, and she is very much in demand. Lauren loves the camera, and she does a lot of fit modeling, mostly for jean companies. Lauren becomes the Lucky Brand fit model and continues to work for other companies as well. As long as modeling does not interfere with her grades, we give her permission to continue modeling.

During Lauren's freshman year at Calabasas, she dates Dusty, a popular, junior, baseball player. They fall in love instantly, and date throughout the high school years. The older girls in Dusty's grade hate Lauren, and are jealous not only of her beauty, but because she wins the heart of one of their peers. Where does she get off dating one of the most popular boys? These girls taunt Lauren on a regular basis, both at school and at parties. The senior girls throw food at her in the lunch room. Lauren begins to hate school, and although she has her own girlfriends, this is a challenge that is overwhelming. Lauren continues to remain on the honor roll, in spite of the fact that she is smoking marijuana and is drinking. This is her escape, especially when the social pressures appear.

Sometimes Lauren will bring Dusty home after school. Ash is also there doing her homework or playing with a friend. I put out snacks to encourage a healthy setting. This works and we have peace throughout the house for a while.

Dusty's parents are hard-working people that live in a modern ranch house. It is a cozy place and Lauren spends a lot of time there. Dusty's mom is an incredible cook and they adore Lauren. We have dinner with their family and a scrumptious roast with all the fixings is served, only to be followed with homemade, delectable, berry pie. No wonder Lauren loves being there. Lauren comes home one day and asks, "Why don't we have a big fruit bowl sitting on our counter?" Off to the store I go to buy and arrange a fruit bowl that even Martha Stewart would envy.

Dusty and Lauren come to our house often, but nevertheless, they are often alone, creating their own party. I find out many years later that they would smoke marijuana after school. Lauren takes a couple of trips with his family, and I do not think she is in any great danger, but at fifteen, a rebellious teenager begins to develop and there is an undeniable anger brewing within her. As soon as she comes home, she marches to her room immediately, puts on loud music, and tunes us out. This is part of the norm. One night when she comes home, I am determined to connect with this person whom I hardly know. As she enters through the front door, I suggest having some tea before bedtime, and with a hostile face looking up at me on the second level, she says, "Go back to your cave. I don't want to have anything with you. You're on my back all the time about my curfew, and I hate being here."

In high school, Lauren has a couple of incidents with rules and regulations, but overall she performs well academically and has many close friends. Lauren relates well to the school counselor and the administration. Later, the Vice Principal, Mr. Misel writes the following reference letter for college:

Lauren has consistently exhibited academic achievement during her two years at Calabasas High School. Her ability to deal with various teaching strategies and learning modalities along with old-fashioned hard work has lead her to be a successful student.

On a personal level, Lauren has a highly engaging personality which quickly endears her to people of all ages. Her ability to both work with people and to "stand alone" when necessary is a tribute to her system of basic human values. She is one of those people who see value from helping others. When she walks into a room, it brightens with her brilliant personality. It is my belief that Ms. Zussman will mature into an outstanding young woman.

Mr. Misel is precise with his observations on two counts: Lauren's ability to relate to people of all ages and her compassion to help others in need. This is her passion in life. What Mr. Misel does not report is Lauren's drive for partying and socializing with friends.

Lauren's interest in sports starts to fade and she attends more parties on the weekend. We do not know the extent of her drinking and smoking during her high school years. We had no idea how serious her drinking would become, until many years later.

David starts a new internet business that requires him to be in Las Vegas Monday through Thursday; however, he is always home for the weekends. Subsequently, Lauren told me later during her sober years that she felt abandoned and alone. When David comes home and tries to reunite with his daughter, she yells at the top of her lungs, "You are only my birth father!"

David and I have a strained relationship with Lauren and I find it hard being both parents during the week. As her hostility grows, she gravitates more and more towards Dusty and his family. I am losing my daughter, as her rage and anger are escalating. I recall locking my bedroom door one night, as I hear her ranting, clearly in a fit of anger, slamming her door, shouting out obscenities.

Lauren agrees to see a doctor. She knows she is angry and unhappy. She is tired of fighting with classmates and her family. It is obvious that self-loathing exists within her weak and tired spirit. I ache observing her pain and angst.

After seeing a psychiatrist, Lauren is diagnosed with depression. Attention deficient disorder is also an underlying problem, but I think it is free floating anxiety.

In spite of the therapy, the distance grows between us. I shop at the grocery store with a knot in my stomach. I feel the strain every day, but don't know what to do. My life is falling apart and I realize that you are only as happy as your least happy child.

Ash is doing pretty well overall and is easy to be with. With all the drama in the house over Lauren and her behavior, the other sibling has a lot to deal with. Ash observes a lot of negative behavior between Lauren and me. She, too, misses her father. She is my buddy at night and we make our dinners together, discussing the day's events. Sometimes Lauren joins us; sometimes she takes her food to her room.

I now suspect Lauren is smoking marijuana and I know her peers use too. Unfortunately, it is all too common at her high school. I feel her pain as soon as she walks through the door after school. Self-medicating is not the answer, but her pain and rage draw her to a self-destructive behavior. I am sick with worry and I don't know what to do. How can I reach out to her? How can I bring her back? She and her father hardly communicate and she isn't around very much. It is an unhappy period in our lives. Game boards and movie night do not exist anymore. David is so busy and overwhelmed that he doesn't know if he is coming or going. The dysfunctional aura of our home takes center stage, as my anxiety mounts. I am angry that David is not here to fix the problem, but he needs to make a living. I have many sleepless nights, feeling like a failure as a mother and wife. David wants us to move to Las Vegas, but that is out of the question. The girls and I do not want to leave our neighborhood or our home, and Las Vegas is not a place to raise our children. I feel he is not home long enough to unite with our family, even though he drives home every weekend.

I begin therapy, as I am not only a Stepford Wife, but an unsuccessful one. I am going through the motions of running a model home. Meals are planned, beds are made and everything is in perfect order. The picture looks good but we are struggling and our family unit is disengaging day by day.

One day after school, Lauren and three girlfriends are sitting in a parked car in front of her high school. A police officer pulls up and has the girls step out of the car. The girls are just chatting, yet the officer is suspicious. He asks to search Lauren's purse and she agrees with no Miranda rights or search warrant. The officer proceeds to search Lauren's make up bag and finds a bud of marijuana. Another girl also has a pipe in her bag. Both girls get busted and are issued a ticket. We are off to court within weeks to handle this red-flag situation. Lauren tells us she was holding this bud for "a friend."

Lauren's Uncle Marc, an attorney, handles the case, which is dismissed due to the lack of a search warrant and no Miranda rights. Had Lauren been convicted, she would have lost her driver's license, and would not have been able to get to school or work.

After this incident, I have her drug tested. The first time she argues with the positive results, claiming that it was from the smoke in her friend's car or the smoke from the parties she attends. The next test comes out positive and she doesn't deny it. The more we pull the reins in, the more she rebels.

One night I notice that Lauren has something shiny on her tongue when she is speaking. It is a tongue ring. Tongue piercing is new and we do not approve of this fad. When we insist she take out her tongue ring, she fights with us, tooth and nail. We finally tell her the tongue ring goes, or she has to leave. She replies, "Fuck you," and she is out the door. Hours later, we are driving up and down the street, in a police car, looking for our tongue-pierced daughter. Finally, Lauren comes home and her father convinces her to take it out. Lauren asks him to save it for her because she has an emotional attachment to it. He agrees and puts it in the safe.

On a warm summer day, while David is attending to business in Las Vegas, we have an intervention. Lauren is fifteen years old and is prescribed an amphetamine for depression by a competent psychiatrist–so I thought. Dr. S. is a savvy man, in his fifties with a heavy mustache, who relates well to teenagers. He has a teasing, quiet, seductive demeanor that somewhat entertains Lauren. The interaction is a good dance, as I observe the two of them conversing. After a few sessions, Dr. S. consults with David and me. "Lauren is between a fifteen and a twenty-five-year-old woman. Her complex thoughts swing back and forth and it amazes me. This lack of integration keeps her from feeling grounded. She seems depressed and needs medication." What teenager is really grounded? However,

I wonder how much is she is using and drinking. How effective and how safe is the medication? I trust the doctor.

During this time on medication, Lauren's weight drops ten pounds and I notice her bony shoulders pointing out of her white t-shirt. Her energy soars with productive work and a new sense of liveliness, but after a couple of weeks, I notice a surge of anger and rage. After we come home from an out-of-town weekend, I observe a perfectly cleaned room. Lauren has gone on a cleaning marathon, and she has replaced all our family framed pictures with pictures of her and her friends. I find this odd and I make her change them back.

A few weeks later, I am home upstairs and I hear a commotion downstairs. Ash comes in through the front door screaming. I run out to the hallway, only to find Lauren following Ash, fully charged. Her glassy eyes are filled with rage, as she throws a bottle at Ash. I realize that Lauren is totally out of control and I fear she will seriously hurt Ash. Immediate intervention is necessary and I call 911. Frozen in fear, I now call David several times, but he has to meet a client due in from Europe. I contact her psychiatrist and he sets up another appointment to assess the situation, but not soon enough. Meanwhile, 911 sends backup and help arrives shortly. Before I know it, I have a squad team wearing orange jackets in my living room, including a drug intervention counselor. This husky, blonde woman is the only one who can speak to Lauren about surrendering.

Sitting on her balcony, off her bedroom, Lauren is quiet while the counselor speaks softly. "Lauren, no one wants to hurt you. We want to help you. Your mom told us that your medicine is making you do things you wouldn't normally do. Please let us help you. You are out of control and we need to take you to the hospital so you won't hurt anyone, including yourself." The woman's strong, deep-toned voice is soothing, yet authoritative.

The ambulance pulls up without the siren, but the neighbors are watching this dramatic event. I know what they are thinking. "It must be one of the Zussman girls." I am now in a complete tizzy, as a good neighbor comes over to take Ash to their house.

Lauren remains in a calm state, somewhat detached from the counselor, but also conversing. I know not to interfere, as a stranger has a more influential hand to promote Lauren's cooperation. Sadness sets in and her eyes are no longer glassy. Lauren's long, exhausted face tells a story of waiting to be rescued. "How long can I tap dance through this madness? When will I have relief from my depression and anxiety? Who can help me? Where is my dad–the dad that always rooted me on at my soccer games? I hate everybody! I hate myself." I call David and the psychiatrist to give them a heads up.

Finally, Lauren agrees to enter the ambulance. David's meeting is the next morning. He drops everything and heads for the airport. I am paralyzed with fear and drive myself to the U.C.L.A. psychiatric hospital. Where did my daughter go and how did it come to this? This is the pivotal point of identifying a teenager in dire need of good professional help and support from her family. My baby is in serious trouble. We are a team. I will not give up–not now, not ever.

I enter the admission's entrance and they have Lauren in a back room. Her father is on his way to the hospital after landing at the airport. I call my mother, who criticizes me for initiating this intervention. Grandma can't imagine how dangerous the situation is, as we did not tell her about Lauren's escalating rage and out of control behavior.

The nurse approaches me and leads me to Lauren's room behind white, stark drapes. She pulls the drapes back and I see my girl listening to her walkman, tuning everything and everyone out. In a passive, calm state Lauren glances at me, as I softly speak. "Honey, I had to do this. You need help, and we are here to support you. You won't stay long, just long enough to get this under control. Daddy is on his way." Half listening, she continues to nod her head to the music, almost in a dream-like state. By this time, her dreary eyes barely can stay open, and she lets me rub her back. I now pat her forehead and stroke her hair. She holds one of my hands and smiles. She suddenly seems like an innocent child, looking up to me, after a bad case of the flu. A piercing pain stabs at my heart as I realize how much she is suffering.

Suddenly, David enters the room. He might have had a superman outfit with a cape and a big S on his chest. It is now seven o'clock and we have been here for a couple of hours. "Hi, baby, how ya doing?"

Lauren continues to listen to her music but now takes her daddy's hand. She doesn't speak, but an immediate calmness comes across her face, and she smiles because she knows she is finally safe.

Daddy was there to calm the seven-year old as she was stitched up. Lauren fell off the handlebars and her tooth pierced through her lower lip. There were also many nights spent using a medical nebulizer to relieve Lauren's breathless asthma. Daddy was *always* there and would carry his girl to the outside backyard to get fresh, cold air into her lungs. We also had many trips to the emergency room, when Lauren would accidentally eat pine nuts–a life and death allergy. All in all, Daddy was there when she needed him, and in Lauren's eyes, the man could move mountains.

A doctor soon enters and tells us she will be observed for seventy-two hours. We sign the necessary forms and she willingly agrees to stay. Tearfully, I say goodbye and we all exchange hugs. David and I walk out of the hospital, and I break down like an overflowing dam. He has to fly out to Las Vegas the next morning, to meet the client from Switzerland, and will return shortly. We are close during this time. No blame, no anger–we just hug each other with sadness and helplessness. Our girl is in trouble.

The next day, I enter the UCLA psychiatric floor of young girls, mostly anorexic-looking. I am allowed to go through metal locked doors after a buzzer is rung. Eating disorders are big on this floor, as I see many teens sadly wasting away. The different forms of mental illness swirl around my head and put me in a hypnotic trance for a few moments. Is our girl really here? I feel like I am hallucinating in a sea of troll dolls. It is a surreal environment, one that is foreign to me, except in movies. Lauren greets me as if it is a day at camp. I am relieved, but surprised. Being claustrophobic, a residual from being in the MGM hotel fire, I focus my eyes on the window. *I can do this.*

Lauren sits down and quietly tells me the story on each girl. "Mom, these girls are mostly anorexic. No one wants to eat around here. The food is pretty good, but the nurses stand behind everyone and write down what we eat. No problem with me. I ate my plate and the girl's plate next to me. Put away power." She smiles, as I am surprised at how she has adjusted to the environment. "The girl in the purple shirt took an overdose of her mother's pills. She is back for a second time. The girl behind her tried to kill herself, too. Pretty fucked up, huh?" It suddenly seems like a slumber party, but in a Stephen King book. I smile, as she seems to be the old Lauren. I pat her head of long chestnut-brown hair, and she continues her report. "We have classes and I am working on a painting. I did it this morning." Lauren takes me to an area where there is an art room.

Many incomplete paintings are on easels. Wheels of colored oil paints are on a rustic wood table with paint brushes and sponges. The smell of paint and turpentine permeates the room. Lauren proudly shows her painting of a field with wild flowers, all in vivid multi-colors. I am impressed as I admire the deep shades of blue, turquoise and green. I smile broader as she reads my face of pleasure. "It is beautiful – a true work of art," I tell her. I take a deep breath and we return to the lounge area. It surprises me to witness an enthusiastic patient, with no urgency to leave. She seems calm and very sweet only to hold my hand as we walk around.

I tell her I have an appointment with Dr. M. Lauren tells me she has seen him this morning and last night. I try to encourage her to talk about the meeting, but to no avail. She continues, "We have rules here but everyone kinda does their own thing. They watch you when you go to the bathroom –weird, huh? A woman came to talk to me wearing a long white coat. I don't know who she was, but she asked a lot of questions." My ears perk up again, but I don't want to pry. I imagine this woman asking her if she hates her mother and did I cause this? This has to be my fault completely, and I am not fit for this world. My "Woody Allen" voice continues to tell me I could also take some personality classes and I don't deserve to be this girl's mother or anyone's mother.

My appointment with Dr. M. approaches as it is two o'clock in the afternoon. I am already exhausted, but perk up as I enter his cherry wood office. I sit down in front of his desk and I feel like I am visiting the school principal. I view a picture of his blonde, smiling wife and young children. It could be a Christmas card picture, and it is obvious that this is a happy bunch. I bet his kids won't end up here. Good genes.

The doctor enters the room and he greets me with a sympathetic but cheerful greeting. He has sandy-colored hair and a clean-cut appearance and can easily be mistaken for a doctor in a soap opera. The medication is immediately eliminated, as it seems to be the culprit here. Other options are discussed and Lauren is prescribed a new antidepressant. Dr M. tells me that she is not in any great danger and the medication will soon be completely out of her body. Clearly, an amphetamine was a poor choice. She can be released today, before the seventy-two hour hold. I am relieved, sign the necessary papers for release, and I return to Lauren's floor to tell her the good news.

The metal doors reopen and I am calmer about the institutional setting. Who said exposure therapy doesn't work? It is my second time around. I see Lauren and we sit on a sofa for two, away from the wandering patients.

"Lauren, the doctor said you can go home and you will be taking new medication."

She doesn't look surprised. "What about my art? I am not done."

"Don't you want to go home?" I ask.

"I want to finish my painting." Suddenly, she looks like a little girl in a safe environment. I remember her painting, wearing a cherry-print smock, with her hair in pigtails.

"You can take the painting home and finish it."

"Okay, but I really started to like it here."

I hug her and she hugs me back. We gather her things and check out. I think Lauren's addictive behavior was part of the problem, and the medication prescribed invited her to abuse the dosage. Looking back, it was like adding oil to fire - fire that was smoldering within her. She felt elated with this medication, so why not double the dose, or even triple it? Trusting the medication and the psychiatrist is a whole other story.

I had a very dear friend in Chicago during my single days. Esther was my neighbor when I lived along the outer drive of the north side of Chicago. Our adventures were typical of two single girls during the '70s. Rush Street, dancing, drinking and dating new men were all the norms during the weekends.

Esther was a drug addict. Unfortunately, after years of abuse, she couldn't sustain sobriety. Esther later developed epilepsy, and eventually died from complications at age 42. Living many years in California, I was devastated when I learned of her death, especially since I knew she was in rehab twice.

Lauren was twelve years old when I learned about Esther's untimely death. She knew we were best friends and entered my bedroom upon me learning the news. As tears rolled down my cheeks, I explained that Esther's death was a real tragedy, and that her failed recovery made her spiral down to a destructive world of addiction. Knowing this, I could not blame Esther for her weakness, but realized that this addiction was bigger than what she could tackle. King Kong got the better of my dear friend. There was no need for judgments, just love. As I explained this to Lauren, I also warned her about the downfall of drugs and alcohol. Little did I know that my daughter would later follow in my best friend's footsteps, battling addiction.

When Lauren was in the hospital, I thought about Esther and how drugs can destroy a life. Even in Dr. M's office, I comprehended the complexities of drug intake, especially for an adolescent, whether legal or illegal. Yet, antidepressants can not only save a life, but can also improve the quality of life.

Back home, things actually return to normal: new therapist, new medication. I read Lauren's diary, looking for drugs or alcohol usage but I find nothing in the written word. My fifteen-year-old goes back to her life in Calabasas–school dances, girlfriend parties, but mostly with Dusty at his parents' house. I realize that my girl is part child, part woman. How did this happen? We were just at Mommy and Me. David returns home, no longer commuting to Las Vegas, and our family life resumes to a stable, normal lifestyle.

Lauren gets along with her teachers, but hates high school, primarily because of the constant, tedious social pressures. The older girls continue to bully her. Because of Lauren's extra credits, she bypasses her last two years of high school and passes the high school proficiency test. This allows her to enter Junior College at age 16. I am not thrilled about this idea, but I know the social conflict at school contributes to her desperate need to escape. At this time, the storm seems to subside, and she is looking forward to college.

At 16, Lauren is still dating Dusty and we decide to move to Newport Beach, ninety minutes from Calabasas. Ash is just starting high school and Lauren is entering Junior College. David and I both have business opportunities and we love living by the water. After the devastating earthquake and the uncomfortable heat of the valley, it is time to make a change. The girls do not like this, but we promise to continue to maintain the old friendships. Lauren reluctantly moves and soon breaks up with Dusty. The relationship has taken its course and the long distance driving only makes things worse.

When she starts school at Orange Coast College, Lauren meets her new best friend, Jessica, a beautiful blonde classmate. Going to parties and hanging out is a ritual on weekends. Jessica becomes our third daughter, and we watch "Betty and Veronica" (the comic book icons), in the school play. That's what they call themselves, because one is blonde and the other is a brunette. They are actually very good actresses. Jess is a serious actress and had a part on the soap opera, *General Hospital.* Lauren isn't really serious about acting even though we will pay for her acting lessons years later in L.A. Jess is a party girl, but she is a good girl. She has a typical, uneventful teenage life. Drugs and alcohol are not really in the picture, nor is sleeping around. The girls are stunning, dressed up in their nightclub gear, but again, I do not think they were in harm's way.

At this point, I have to give up control and let the girls develop their own lives. David and I are now very busy with our careers. Besides, controlling Lauren is impossible and provokes arguments.

Before long, Jess and Lauren are driving to L.A. to hit the Hollywood clubs and parties. Their connections and beauty get them through the VIP doors, and soon they are with many well-known celebrities.

I become suspicious when a limo from L.A. comes to pick up the girls. Yet, Lauren is getting good grades and she is modeling regularly. Jess comes from a nice family and I trust her. So what am I afraid of? I am afraid of the usual rapes, drugs, and rock and roll that go on behind the scenes. Lauren constantly argues with us that she is responsible and that she and Jess are safe. Don't forget, I am a mother and all this fluff doesn't sit right with me; however, we allow these weekends to continue. Sometimes Lauren and Jess would spend the night in L.A. I have many sleepless nights but she does call to tell us she is safe. Considering she is drinking and partying, I don't know how she continues to get good grades. There are many weeknights of studying and writing papers, but the weekends are reserved for the good times.

Malibu parties and invitations to events continue to circulate with the "in crowd". Lauren is headed for trouble, as the excessive weekend drinking continues.

৩৽

CHAPTER 4

Lake Havasu: The Turning Point

"If you are not in the state of acceptance, enjoyment or enthusiasm, look closely and you will find that you are creating suffering for yourself and others."

Eckhart Tolle

Lake Havasu is a popular vacation spot for the younger generation to party, and the Memorial Day weekend is no exception. This lake is located on the California and Arizona border and is a party playground with no limits. Boozing and drugging is the norm and all hell usually breaks loose. At 18, Lauren is ready to escape and party hard.

I do not know the extent of the madness. Lauren and Jessica meet their friends on a boat for an adventurous rendezvous. There is no limit to alcohol and drugs as the weekend progresses on and off the boat. Under the hot sun for hours, Lauren consumes twelve beers (yes, twelve) and some marijuana.

It is the eve of Memorial Day. Lauren is outside a local bar and passes out, face down in the dirt. Jessica and a couple of friends find Lauren and cannot wake her. Panic starts to set in, for they all know she is in serious trouble. They decide to drive her to the local hospital, drop her off, and dodge the legal entanglement that will follow.

Lauren is still completely unconscious, and remembers doctors pumping on her chest at 5 AM as she awakes. Tubes and I.V.'s are everywhere. She comes to with luck and appropriate interventions. Lauren is released two hours later with a firm lecture from the doctors. Months later, she confesses to going out that same morning to pick up a six-pack of beer, only to party some more.

I receive the phone call from Lauren a couple of hours after her release from the hospital convincing me that someone had spiked her drink at a local bar. She tells me she was briefly hospitalized and they needed to clean her system out with an I.V. The truth of the matter is that she came extremely close to dying due to binge drinking. You read about this happening in college towns and the newspapers frequently report current deaths from this irresponsible, erratic behavior. The only good thing that came from this near-death experience is that it is her final wake-up call. Within 48 hours she is in rehab as an out-patient.

The next day she arrives home, goes to the bank, and recognizes Nick standing in line. Nick is a drug and alcohol counselor who had spoken a couple of months earlier at her college. Little does Lauren know that her guardian angel is there to guide her to a new life. Telling Nick the truth is hard, but she tells him about her near-death experience and he not only convinces her, but orders her to show up at his rehab center at 4:00 PM that afternoon. It works and this is the turning point. Not only does she painstakingly confess to us the real story, but she tells her father and me that she has been an alcoholic since she was fifteen. She cannot control her alcohol intake.

This admission is shocking to both of us, as we had no idea of the extent of her drinking. Lauren could have told us that she wanted a sex change and we couldn't have been more shocked. How did this happen? When did this happen? I was a stay-at-home mom most of the time, or I worked from the house. I knew she dabbled in alcohol and marijuana, like most of her peers, but I had no idea that she was in the serious danger zone, heading to her death.

The next day, Lauren has just had a meeting with Nick. As David and I approach the office, we hear Lauren talking to Nick. I hear Lauren say, "This will break my mother's heart," and it certainly did.

Nick is a 45-year-old, heavy-set man and has a street-smart mentality. He could easily pass for a slick car salesman. He is an ex-addict who now runs this rehab facility in Tustin, just miles from our house. He instantly takes Lauren under his wing and convinces her that she is in desperate need of a Twelve Step intense program.

"Mom, my drink was not spiked."

"What happened?" I ask.

"I was at the bar with Jess and some of my friends and I wanted to get high."

"And…"

Lauren continues in quiet, monotone voice. "And I mixed my soda with HGB. I had been drinking all day."

"What is HGB?"

Nick turns to David and me, eyeball to eyeball, and then delivers the following words. "It is a drug that can slow the heartbeat and breathing, therefore producing a coma or even death."

I can feel my face turning white and David is clearly disturbed as Nick continues. "Respiration depression can be severe enough to require life support. It can easily put a person on a ventilator or breathing machine."

"Holy shit!" is what I am thinking. I am speechless and David is silent. He knows he can't fix this. This is huge, and a very serious problem.

Lauren continues with her confession. "Mom, I have been drinking excessively since I was fifteen. I can't seem to stop. I seem to want more and more, when my friends are able to stop."

David turns to Nick. "What can we do?"

"Your daughter is in trouble. Lauren needs to be here for two weeks as an outpatient."

"Then what does she do?" David asks sheepishly.

"Then she needs to religiously go to a Twelve Step program, everyday." Nick looks at Lauren with piercing eyes. "Are you ready to commit to the program, young lady?"

"Yes, yes I am," she convincingly answers.

How did Lauren manage to pull this off? Was my 18-year-old really an alcoholic? In shock, we attend a parent meeting at the rehab center with other parents that are in the same boat. It is a nightmare evening, with horror stories of these adolescents that have put their parents through Hell. One story tops the other and I think I am at the wrong place. It was just yesterday that we were applying for the preschools, going to ballet classes, and now we are in a parent rehab group. It feels like a poorly written Lifetime movie. Then the realization comes to the surface and slaps us in the face. How did we not know? What about the legal mess over the marijuana bud in her purse? What about the sneakiness and running around? What about hanging out with the Hollywood gang and disappearing on weekends? Were we too permissive—too trusting?

David and I have a serious talk and decide to write a letter to Lauren that clearly states what we will *not* tolerate. Being the responsible parent, David writes the following and signs both of our names.

June 16, 2000
Dear Lauren,

We want to discuss the changes to your current lifestyle that you are going to make if you want to continue to live at home for free, and drive the Mustang car that I pay for, including the maintenance, repairs, gas and insurance.

You have been making bad decisions regarding your life and choosing your friends. We will not tolerate your drinking and using drugs. You are not acting like a responsible adult.

We will not enable you to continue partying, running around all night, sleeping all day, and leaving your room looking like a pig pen. You need to clean your dirty clothes weekly and keep your room clean.

You need to help around the house, instead of fighting with everyone. You talk on the phone for hours (per your home phone bill that I pay) and you are disrespectful to us.

I will not give you money to move out this summer so you can run to clubs and parties. When you go to a four-year college, we will pay for your classes, books, food and dorm. If you don't want to follow these rules, then you need to move out, get a full-time job and pay for your rent, food and car expenses.

WE LOVE YOU – but we will not help you kill yourself.
Mom and Dad

The group preaches about not enabling our children. We need to put our foot down and insist on sobriety, but in reality, it is up to the individual to choose sobriety. The leader tells us to take the tough-love approach. The relapse rate is high, but not if one commits to sobriety. We leave the meeting feeling numb and frightened, but at the same time optimistic. We are also thankful to have this intervention. Through luck and incredible dedication to the program, Lauren never wavers. She is going to be a winner in the program, and she is entering a new phase that allows her a second chance at life.

Alcoholism is an insidious disease, and although it can have a mind of its own, the individual with tenacity wins the battle. It is the time to strip down, without drugs and alcohol, and fight the demons of life. With no practice to fend off the anxiety of life, Lauren is entering a scary phase. She has to delete her past and end lifelong friendships. She has to attend daily meetings. She simply has to face the devil and proceed with the journey of sobriety.

On July 5, 2000, Lauren officially joins the Twelve Step program in our neighborhood. She has a sponsor and attends meetings daily. Leaving her drinking buddies behind and staying away from bars and parties are the hardest things to do. She looks depressed and confused, yet she wakes up in the morning and attends the meetings. Nick sometimes attends the meetings and greets Lauren. Afterward, the group goes to breakfast and mingles. Lauren feels like a fish out of water. This is clearly her darkest hour and the look of bewilderment is written all over her face. *Who are these people? Why can't I hang out with Jess and my friends? The weekend is coming up...what will I do?*

This whole phase involves a total transformation and discipline. Alcoholics are known for their lack of discipline. Lauren knows that she has to surrender to God or a higher power and follow the rules. The world had been Lauren's oyster. There were no real rules, and if there were, there was always someone to rescue her if she broke them. Lauren simply lacked self-discipline. *What is this nonsense about responsibility? Why must I give up the pleasure of drinking?*

The first year of sobriety is the hardest for Lauren, with constant unsettling feelings. How can she deal with life without alcohol? What is she to do when she wants to check out? Well, the answer is simple. Go to a meeting, call your sponsor, write in your journal or put your head between your knees, but do not drink. Lauren refers to herself as a "dry alcoholic." The program saves her life, but it is Hell. There simply isn't any substitute for hard work. Lauren makes new friends in AA and I meet many of them. They are lovely and so kind, with happy faces, all different ages, coming from all walks of life. The older members gravitate toward Lauren and she loves their wisdom. Years later, whenever Lauren comes home from New York, she always meets with them.

This marks the beginning of Lauren's spiritual journey. She reads and digests many books as she tries to find her way, clean and sober. At the same time, a clean diet and healthy exercise become a daily ritual. Daily meetings, journal writing, exercise and spiritual reading, including studying the Twelve Steps, become the norm.

Before my eyes, within months, I see a caterpillar turn into a butterfly; however, many dark days of depression emerge and the pain is excruciating. Even though it is a very challenging time, Lauren manages to take one day at a time. Continuation of modeling and school is only second to attending daily meetings. This is her first priority, as she leaves behind her old friends, and makes new sober ones.

Lauren soon moves to Beverly Hills and modeling becomes a full time job. She rents a beautiful guest house behind The Beverly Hills Hotel. Lauren bonds with Nicki, the woman of the main house, who is very kind and nurturing. The soft-spoken, slender, attractive, middle-aged woman has a European accent. David and I chat with her and we think that this is a lovely residential neighborhood. Most importantly, it seems safe and is in the center of Beverly Hills. The one-room guesthouse is newly constructed and is surrounded with woodsy trees. It is a perfect place to meditate and journal write, as meditation along with yoga become a regular practice for Lauren.

Yoga and meditation are good substitutes for drugs and alcohol. They train the body to rely on its natural resources. They quiet the mind and soothe the soul. The more you practice, the more they become natural to the self. It is a new awakening, and Lauren takes to this unfamiliar way of life, in spite of the uncomfortable regular visits of depression and anxiety.

Against her doctor's suggestion, she refuses to take a non-addicting antidepressant. Toughing it out is the only way for her to win this battle of addiction, at this time. However, David and I worry when Lauren goes to a dark place, and stays in bed for three days. Her sister Ash drives up from San Diego, a three hour ride, to help her sister. They are always there for each other, especially when one is in any kind of trouble. Ash stays with Lauren through this dark time. Lauren's depression eventually lifts and work keeps her busy.

Meetings are still her major priority and sober new friends come into the picture. However, Lauren thinks the Beverly Hills crowds are very plastic, in spite of their recovery. Many members are actors, actresses, or in the industry, with huge egos to match. Men continuously hit on Lauren, even though it is discouraged by the Twelve Step program. Lauren would often be asked at Hollywood parties what she did for a living. Most assumed she was in the movie or modeling industry. She would answer with a straight face, "I clean houses for a living and really enjoy it. It's good therapy." Lauren had a great sense of humor and protected herself well. Even when she was a top model, she would tell people that she was in the fashion industry, which could have meant a lot of things.

January 31, 2003 is Lauren's 21st birthday, and she is three years sober. It is a delightful, warm, sunny day, unusual for the winter months. Most of her contemporaries would be celebrating a drunken weekend in Las Vegas. This is what twenty-one-year-olds usually do–drink. So what can Lauren do to celebrate? I decide to take the day off of work and take my Toots to the Bel Air Hotel.

David and I surprise Lauren after we pick her up from her Beverly Hills apartment. The breathtaking grounds of the Bel Air Hotel, among the mansions and winding roads, faintly bring back memories from her childhood days when we dined there regularly for holidays. The eucalyptus trees, sprawling plants, and fragrant, colorful flowers are a breathtaking sight. Living an hour away for the last ten years has kept this gem of a place at a distance. Its woodsy location is surrounded by a beautiful pond with white water lilies floating alongside wild ducks and swans. Many weddings are performed around the water and it is a well known location for celebrities. Valet parkers greet us and whirl our car away. David and I instinctively know this is a place that will win Lauren's heart. She instantly loves this beauty of a landmark. She drifts around the pond in her brown, gypsy-style skirt, her typical Bohemian way to dress, as her wide smile tells us we made the right choice. We take some pictures with Lauren's drugstore disposable camera. Total joy embraces her.

We stroll fifty feet away to the elegant restaurant, and we are immediately seated in a circular, red leather booth, viewing the tuxedo-dressed waiters serving sparkling water and fine wines. The snow-colored Casablanca lilies with overgrown white baby's breath branches compliment the floral arrangements throughout the restaurant.

Eating our salads and tasting each other's food, we make our typical food noises that would probably be annoying to others: umm, ooh, taste this. Of course there is no champagne, and it isn't missed, as we are truly in paradise.

After pitchers of iced tea, I dash to the bathroom, and upon returning I notice Oprah Winfrey and two men sitting in the booth next to ours. How can that be? Although we see celebrities from time to time, this is a bit overwhelming and Lauren can't believe it. Lauren has met many celebrities and has been in their Malibu and Bel Air homes; however, this is Ms. O. and like everyone else in the world, Lauren has a spiritual connection with the iconic talk host via satellite.

I whisper to the family that it is indeed Ms. O. Soon Oprah learns that it is Lauren's milestone birthday. We respect Oprah's privacy, even though we are about to pee in our pants. When Oprah finishes her meal, she appears in front of our table, greets us with a big smile, and wishes Lauren a happy birthday. Lauren tells Oprah how much she and her mom admire her shows and that her mom is from Chicago. Oprah, viewing a camera on our table, insists on taking some pictures with the birthday girl, not that she had to twist her arm. We step away from our booth and the camera begins flashing. We all have our pictures taken and then Lauren takes some shots with Oprah–pictures, not alcohol.

Oprah assumes Lauren is a model and after inquiring, she says to her, "What is it like living in Beverly Hills, being a beautiful model?" To Oprah's surprise and without batting an eye, Lauren states, "Oh Oprah, I have demons. Life isn't so easy." They chat briefly about why people lack happiness in spite of all their possessions, beauty and wealth.

Oprah speaks about her new school in Africa, and Lauren wants to know why these children are so happy, when in reality, they have very little. Lauren inquires about the children of Africa being so happy just playing with a ball, while our children in America are so miserable. The conversation continues, as we watch the interaction of a real conversation about life and values. I am watching a verbal tennis match, speechless and dumbfounded. Lauren tells Oprah that sobriety is hard, especially in this town.

They both cover so much in such a short period of time, and they exchange phone numbers upon departing. We say our goodbyes. Within minutes Oprah comes back to our booth and announces that she is taking our daughter away with her. (What a birthday!) I have no idea where they go, but David and I continue our lunch as time goes by. We drink many cups of coffee, and yet there is no sign of Lauren. Did they go shopping? Leave the grounds? Where is my daughter, and what better way to celebrate a birthday?

Lauren tells us later that she and Oprah wander off to a private garden on the grounds and have a profound conversation about their past lives. Heart-to-heart, soul-to-soul, cortex-to-cortex, it is a "no bullshit" conversation. Depression, alcoholism, sobriety, and everyday struggles are just some of the topics they discuss. Could her twenty-first birthday be any more exciting than to not only meet Oprah, but to converse on the deepest, most meaningful level? What a gift!

A week later, Oprah calls my house looking for Lauren. Of course I think it is one of my friends playing a joke on me until I realize this really is Oprah. Lauren's cell phone is broken and for whatever reason, Lauren does not call Oprah back immediately. Lauren wants to complete her journey of sobriety before she contacts her. Although they never reconnect, Lauren tells me that one day, when she develops her inner voice to be a national speaker; she will indeed cross paths once again with Oprah. She feels that she is still a bud, waiting to someday bloom into a flower, with gifts that are to come. Lauren simply needs more time to grow and experience her spiritual awakening on a broader level. Lauren never bragged about this experience.

After Lauren's passing, I send Oprah the article from the *LA Times - Daily Pilot,* about Lauren's journey, with a letter reminding Oprah of that incredible day. I also send a picture of the two of them taken that glorious day. A couple of weeks later, we receive a hundred globe-shaped, pink peonies with a letter, remembering Lauren and all that she represents. It is quite an honor, and a bittersweet day realizing that this experience has come full circle. I cry with a smile on my face. I hope Lauren is smiling from above and knows that Ms. O is thinking of her.

OPRAH WINFREY

December 3, 2008

Lynda and David Zussman
150 Lessay
Newport Beach, CA 92657

Dear Lynda and David,

I'm so sorry to hear of Lauren's passing. She was a light force because I remember the day we met. (I meet hundreds of people that I've forgotten by the end of the day). I was struck by her positive joy field.

I know that as you continue to grieve her passing you feel even closer to her in spirit.

May you be comforted and blessed by her light.

I think Lauren spoke from her heart with Oprah and that is why and how this connection happened. Lauren was comfortable talking to all kinds of people, even famous people, because she was guileless. She was once invited to a small sit down dinner to honor the late and famous Johnny Carson. Not only did Lauren not know who Mr. Carson was (because this famous celebrity was before her time), but she asked him innocently about his journey, spoken like a wise sage—our "no bullshit" girl.

As time goes by, Beverly Hills and the L.A. crowd seem empty to Lauren. She keeps meeting the same people with the same faces that have no real substance. Wanting more, she realizes it is an ego-driven town and of course, being in the modeling industry, she attracts many artificial people that lack integrity.

During this time, Lauren and I fly to New York for a modeling job. She falls in love with the city. The people, restaurants and energy are unlike those found in any other place, and she needs a change. It is time for her to spread her wings and move to the Big Apple. Although I understand her desire to move, I want to keep her close to me. I quietly feel sad that we will not see her regularly, even though I know she is just a phone call away. More work is offered and she meets new people from all walks of life. The multicultural city appeals to her greatly and she welcomes the challenge of a new life.

I remember when Lauren made the exact decision to move to New York. After driving down to Newport Beach on a Sunday afternoon, her melancholy mood is apparent to both David and me. We read the restlessness in her sad, brown eyes as we sit at the dining room table.

"I am lonely in Beverly Hills, and it seems so superficial. It is the same people, the same parties, the same guys."

"What do you mean?" I asked.

"The people are all about Hollywood, and there is something missing, with the constant theme of unhappiness, of searching, of living a non-productive life, with no meaning." She continues, "They are empty shells, always searching on a meaningless path."

David listens, as she is reaching out for his advice. She always admires her father's words of wisdom. David grew up in Los Angeles, and while going to college supported himself as an extra in movies and commercials. Although he was successful, he never really wanted to be an actor.

After appearing in various series and movies with one or two lines, he was cast in a permanent series called *He and She* starring Richard Benjamin and Paula Prentiss. David was the next door neighbor, a fireman. The show didn't last, but he had a taste of Hollywood and the shallowness of the business. He worked almost daily, often having a couple of lines. After making a national beer commercial, and modeling his hands by lighting the match in the series *Mission Impossible,* it became a bit boring.

David advises Lauren with words of experience, "It is really a dead-end career, even if you sometimes get work, and the people are usually drifters with giant egos."

"You're not kidding," Lauren adds.

"I am glad I went to law school and took a different direction in my life. Maybe it's time to spread your wings and go to New York."

That is all I had to hear. Lauren often talked about the move, but it is a bit much for me to comprehend. The look in her eyes suddenly changes, with hope and desire. Her face seems to soften and a glee starts to emerge when she outlines her new plan to make the move. "Maybe I can try it and transfer my work out there. I love visiting the city with Mom. I need a change."

Within weeks we are packing up her studio apartment, separating boxes to keep in our storage garage and boxes to send to her as soon as she lands an apartment. A friend that she met in L.A. offers his apartment for three weeks while he is vacationing in Europe.

Fear ebbs and flows for Lauren, as the excitement grows. Knowing a few people, she has a place to stay for a couple of weeks until she finds her own place. I picture an innocent fawn, being hit by bright headlights as she explores this new territory. At times she feels it is a bit overwhelming, but she welcomes the challenge. It produces growth, and with growth comes experience, and with growth and experience comes wisdom.

❦

CHAPTER 5

New York, New York: Life in the Big Apple

"Great music, architecture, art, poetry, drama, dance, philosophy, and religion are there for anyone to see as examples of how harmony can be imposed on chaos."

Mihaly Csikszentmihalyi

It is August 2003, a hot and humid week in New York, as Lauren arrives in knee high boots. A phone call later that day tells us she didn't pack enough summer clothes and she needs to buy some sun dresses to survive the heat. While staying with a friend, she finds an apartment with two roommates in SoHo.

A trip to Bloomingdale's is first on her agenda to buy a much-needed mattress. Simultaneously, New York has a complete blackout, as Lauren shops for sun dresses and mattresses. Women are screaming since 9/11 is fresh on everyone's mind. A phone call later conveys how fearless Lauren was during this commotion. "We were told to leave the store and I found this adorable sundress on the sale rack for fifteen dollars. The clerk told me to use the stairwell, and leave the store immediately. I thought she was a drama queen. I am so upset about not getting the dress. I don't understand why everyone was hysterical."

Fearlessness and adventurousness are my daughter's nature, unless it is related to internal fear. External fear usually doesn't exist. During my sleepless nights, as Lauren begins her new life in New York, I think about Marlo Thomas, from the series *That Girl* as a strong woman character, thriving in a city as a single and successful role model. However, that series was in the '60s. City life has changed drastically. Lauren calls me one evening after she settles in.

"The new neighborhood is lonely," she whispers in a sweet low voice. "I miss you, Daddy and Ash so much."

I try to give her encouragement, but there is an ache in my heart. "Give it time, honey. You need some time to adjust."

Soon, the new AA meetings make the city less lonely, as she immediately begins to make new friends. The energy and the excitement bring new hope and joy to her life. Although she has two difficult roommates, she manages to get along with them.

"Many nights, strange men sleep on the living room couch. My roommates have uninvited guests in the apartment. I thought I was living with two girls, not four people. I never know who I am going to bump into when I go to the bathroom in the middle of the night, and some of these dudes are scary."

I start to think about Jack the Ripper and all the Manson-like characters. "Lauren, can you move out?"

"Mom, apartments are hard to find; this isn't the right time."

After hearing this, I order David to go retrieve her and bring her back home. The womb is calling her name, but she does not care. In spite of the roommate situation, Lauren's excited voice tells me everything. Weeks go by and she is definitely adjusting to the city.

"The food and the people are incredible."

"How's work?" I ask.

"I am getting sent out for jobs that I get on the first interview."

"Great! What are the people like that you are meeting?"

"People are different here. They don't care about Hollywood. They have real jobs and real careers. I love the East Coast."

I know she is making this her new home and she won't be back. Not for a long time, maybe years, maybe never. I had to encourage this new journey and not think of my empty nest. I have a career, a loving husband, and another daughter, yet I long for Lauren to come home and to somehow put her in my pocket.

Fortunately, Lauren has a great AA sponsor, Donna, who is a firm but gentle guide. Donna is from Chicago and has many years of sobriety. She is a tough cookie who knows the ropes, not only of the city, but also the challenges of a recovering alcoholic. You can't fool Donna, a no-bullshit sponsor, and you can't fool an ex-manipulator. She's just what Lauren needs.

Soon after arriving in New York, Lauren sprints down the street, one humid evening in August. A cab pulls up to the curb and a dark-haired, tall, young man jumps out of the cab and approaches Lauren. Shocked but intrigued, she converses with this gentleman, who persuades her to have a coffee date the following evening. His alluring, green eyes and gentle demeanor do not send out any red flags.

The next night, after talking for hours across the street from the coffee house, this stranger by the name of Michael convinces Lauren to go on a family trip. Michael's parents are from Connecticut and they immediately take to Lauren upon meeting her. A private jet takes this family to the Bahamas, only to board their private yacht. After inquiring about Lauren's favorite foods, lamb chops and fresh, organic vegetables are served on fine china. This is the beginning of a whirlwind relationship that will grow into love.

As the weeks and months pass, Lauren and Michael continue to go on weekend jaunts, usually with his parents. Sometimes it is a get-away to Florida or a sports game across the country. Michael's sister and her husband, a doctor, would also be part of this union. The family is very kind and generous; however, Lauren feels pressure to be perfect and flawless for the family. They invite her to all family functions.

Finally, Lauren tells Michael that she is a recovering alcoholic and attends AA meetings regularly. Having no experience with this challenge, or any knowledge of the twelve step program, Michael tolerates the situation, but does not really understand it. Lauren introduces Michael to a level of spirituality that in itself brings him to new depths in his life. Never having met a girl like this one, he is falling deeper in love with this fascinating woman. Michael tells Lauren in a letter:

You are the first person to teach me to live. You make me feel so present; you make me feel so aware. You have introduced me to my spiritual side, and I feel more in love than I ever thought I could. You have changed me, to want to be a better person. Your outer beauty is undeniable, but more importantly, your heart and soul are the most beautiful I have ever seen.

Yes, they are in love, but as strong as the bond is, it becomes a struggle. They attend weekend workshops, such as Deepak Chopra and others that open a whole new world for Michael. From the start, he knows Lauren is a complex, but colorful girl. A thirst for spiritual wisdom is now part of her constitution and he too wants to go on this trip. Sharing her journey is fascinating, but at the same time confusing. Lauren's old soul is like a fine bottle of aged red wine, and with the emotional intellect evolving comes the darkness of ambiguous feelings about life–growing pains at their best.

Surely she captures his heart, but Lauren starts to hide her dark side of conflict. Meetings and working the twelve steps are a private affair and one that Michael can never share with her. She is striving to build her foundation. This only puts additional stress on the relationship. Hiding and more hiding only adds to her anxiety. After several months, the pressure of showing up for his parents and the limitation of Michael's authentic spirituality end this relationship. This is extremely painful, but Lauren knows she has to focus on loving and guiding herself. This is part of her growth process. Perhaps she met the right person at the wrong time, or perhaps he could never understand the mind of a recovering alcoholic, as Lauren later states.

"Michael was everything a girl would want. He had everything to offer and I really loved him, but yet, he could never really understand the nature of my complex soul."

"I know, honey. I know it hurts."

"I had to hide my weakness, my sad being at times. I had to present myself as a sweet, careful, energetic girlfriend."

I quietly listen as she vents.

"Besides being exhausted from endless hours of work, I had to wear this false face, at all times, especially around his parents. I can't be Susie Creamcheese…the good girl with no darkness. It is too much on my psychic soul. I was suffocating."

"I understand, Lauren."

"But I am suffering."

"I understand."

Although he loves her deeply, it isn't enough. I send her a poem about healthy self-love, hoping it would help.

Love After Love

The time will come
When, with elation,
You will greet yourself arriving
At your own door, in your own mirror,
And each will smile at the other's welcome,
And say, sit here. Eat.
You will love again the stranger who was yourself.
Give wine. Give bread. Give back your heart
To itself, to the stranger who has loved you
All your life, whom you ignored
For another, who knows you by heart.
Take down the love letters from the bookshelf,
The photographs, the desperate notes,
Peel your own image from the mirror.
Sit. Feast on your life.

Derek Walcott

It takes many months for Lauren to get over the break-up. She dates a few men, but keeps them at a distance. When Lauren is intimate, it comes from her soul and this is a piece of her that she guards well. She needs to have a love affair with herself. The journey has just begun. She needs to grow and develop before she can share her life with another–someone who will have to understand her need for independence and self-acceptance.

She masters her sobriety pretty well the next few months with a deeper understanding of who she really is.

"Mom, I am learning to stand on my own two feet. Just moving to New York on my own has given me incredible strength. I am managing my ups and downs pretty well."

"Daddy and I are so proud of you, sweet pea."

Loneliness and missing her family are common experiences but all in all, her new life is groundbreaking for her. It is a true education. Modeling jobs begin to accumulate, and her reputation as a model begins to grow. At one point she has to turn jobs down, due to her busy, hectic schedule. However, going to AA meetings is always her first priority.

During a quiet evening, alone with a cup of tea, Lauren calls me with a revelation, looking back on the experience of love.

"I need to continue to be on my own right now. I have all these responsibilities and most importantly, I need to take care of myself."

"How are you doing this?"

"I am not copping out, but I'm going to meetings, sharing and facing my pain. I am growing up. Even though I could easily shut the world down and not go to meetings, I know that now, more than ever, I must commit to the meetings."

I commend her on this realization, but more importantly, Lauren knows what she needs to sustain a healthy lifestyle. She continues,

"This is not being selfish, but healthy. I need clarity and peace, without suppressing my quest for serenity. I realize that I was giving up a lot for Michael and his family. They were all very good to me, but it wasn't enough."

"How were you doing this?"

"I was pretending to be perfect, careful not to show my weaknesses."

"What made you want to change this?"

"It is more important to continue to find my true self, rather than to please others. As my anxiety increased, it became a wake-up call. I was in the wrong place."

"But I thought you were in love."

"Love is not enough, because the search for my meaningful life has just begun. The separate psychological wall between Michael and me was incredibly painful. The pain now is excruciating, but this realization only came about after several months."

"You mean after the honeymoon was over?"

"Yeah Mom, after the honeymoon was over. We were in the clouds with each other, until the real problems came up. We had to face the music and neither of us were equipped to take it on."

I am very proud of how she is processing this inner conflict, but I hear sadness in her voice that makes me want to fix it. I know I must let her handle this stage of her life. No more babying her. No more notes for her teachers. It is grow up time.

Lauren starts to attend yoga and meditation classes regularly. She writes in her journal and reveals her feelings daily. Of course, the AA meetings are her lifesaver, as she often mentions the benefits outweigh the daily efforts, even in rain, sleet and hail. "Going to a meeting clears my mind. For some reason, whatever I am going through reflects in the guest speaker's speech. It is uncanny, almost eerie, and as the speaker conveys her awakening to the problem, almost through osmosis, I gain that strength to battle my current problem."

This is the process and the value of regular meetings. It is climbing the ladder to a sane, stable life. It takes the need for alcohol away and replaces it with coping mechanisms necessary for sobriety. Lauren tells me that she has to have a regular schedule. "I know that I need a routine. I wake up and usually go to a meeting to set the tone for the day. Then it is work, maybe a yoga class, or meeting a friend for coffee. My evenings are peaceful with music, tea, and maybe painting, or another meeting –all good things that feed my soul."

Lauren has the wonderful opportunity to travel to Italy. She always had a love for this country and she masters the language of Italian. As the model for Proenza Schouler, she often flies to Milan and Naples. This is one of the perks of the business and she loves it. Lauren proudly dons the couture in the showrooms and contributes her ideas. She could have had her own clothing line.

"This is one step higher than New York, with the food, culture and people. It totally stimulates all of my senses. The cheese, figs, olive oil, balsamic vinegar, peppers, and prosciutto are unlike any I have ever tasted. The flowers and colors of this country make me speechless."

This is a sober girl who is using all her senses to experience life, as it should be. This is her way of reaching a healthy, higher plane. I can hear her elation, as she writes or speaks to us, with these incredible observations.

Through her business connections in Milan, Lauren meets two middle-aged couples, all college professors at the local university. She often dines at their homes, with stimulating conversations throughout the evening.

As the ideas about politics, architecture, art and the psychology of human nature are exchanged, the food, although simple, is slowly enjoyed as each course is more delicious than the last. The meats, fruits, homemade breads, and wines circulate the table, as the heated discussions continue.

New guests join the group each time she visits. She uses her Italian as much as possible, as she is quizzed about the American way of life. She is the new ambassador from New York and California, with her perspective and views of the people and the arts.

She is elated and in awe. Lauren states, "Every piece of furniture seems so authentic–like it has a history of its own. If only it could speak–where it came from, and how it arrived. What kings and queens did it service?"

Once, while resting in the lounge area in an oversized bathroom, fit for royalty, Lauren is fixating on a crystal chandelier. She is fascinated with the architecture and beauty of this hotel with its unique marbling and molding. An older, gray-haired woman also sits in the bathroom and converses with Lauren about the history of this chandelier, and how it was retrieved for this classy hotel bathroom. She apparently knows the history specifically, and Lauren is not only enlightened, but pleasingly amused. "Where would I meet an incredible person like this? She is from England and she is a well known psychiatrist who writes books on the human psyche."

As Lauren is speaking in a soft voice, I suddenly realize that this woman must remind her of her Grandma Janet. I imagine that her kindness and words of wisdom dance between them, as the woman uses her soft, small hands to express her poignant ideas and facts. Lauren loves older, wise people and honors their experiences in life. At our local coffee bar, she would often strike up a conversation with the older folks.

Lauren is engrossed for a couple of hours, talking to this sage woman, knowing this experience is one that will stay with her for a lifetime. This was Lauren's passion–to relate, particularly to interesting people about their journeys, their sorrow, their regrets, their joy. It turns out that this woman has a very sick adult son with serious mental illness. Realizing that almost everyone has incredible challenges, Lauren is impressed by the woman's dedication to making life better for herself and her family.

Lauren writes, "There are just some things you can't learn from a textbook. This experience tells me that everyone has the ability to change the course of their fate–to take the tiger by the tail, and tackle whatever life throws you and most of all, appreciate what you do have."

Lauren is very aware of healthy nutrition, and studies the value of food. She eliminates all sugar and white flour from her diet. The diet has to be pure and simple: salmon, eggs, vegetables, olive oil, a little chicken or turkey. Like alcohol, Lauren finds sugar to be addicting and she claims it affects her mood. She announces, "I am hypoglycemic. If I don't have proper protein, I become lightheaded, sometimes shaky." I tell her that she must have gotten that from me. I have to eat protein every four hours. We both take our food very seriously.

Stevia, a sugar substitute, is sprinkled on everything, and she is often teased about this. Wherever we go, Lauren whips out the Stevia from her purse: at home, at restaurants, anywhere she dines. She sprinkles it on veggies, fruits, and to tell you the truth, she would put it on a knuckle sandwich. Her healthy eating is all part of the holistic way to good physical health.

Nourishing the body by choosing the right food is just another way of initiating self-love. This is something that goes along with sobriety–attending to one's physical and mental health. Lauren tells me straight out, "I need proper rest and food to go out there and survive in this world. When I am run down, I weaken, and my defenses go to shit."

Dining out with boyfriends tested these young men. Lemon on the side, salad dressing on the side (particularly olive oil and balsamic vinegar) would be the first request. Always extra veggies on the side, in addition to the regular veggies, no matter what the cost, and in New York, extra veggies can cost you an arm and a leg. No sugar of any kind is another statement. A glass of wine can be ordered by her date, but any more than that becomes an issue. If you smoke, you are history.

Lauren would ultimately have to be herself, continue to feed her soul and have a certain amount of independence. Like the Beverly Hills days of partying and empty shells of people, she knew that New York had their share of superficial people. Some men dashed to her side, only interested in dating a beautiful model. Her radar would go off. Lauren knew this was going to be the caliber of men going to parties and bars in New York, and avoided them. She could read men like a fortune teller could read a palm. She said, "You can't buy milk at the hardware store." Bravo, Toots.

A few years ago, Lauren flies from New York to Chicago to meet us for a big family reunion. Aunts and Uncles join us at a busy, crowded Greek restaurant. There is little to no service. We see a whole pig on a sphere go by and we all laugh. Lauren is so happy to see everyone, and let us not forget the food or the aroma. Not only are her dietary requests granted, but the waiters all come charging to accommodate this beauty of a girl. It is a riot, as all the relatives watch this comedic scene. We can't get water if our lives depend on it, but Lauren just about gets a lemon tree delivered when she asks for a lemon. She always has a wide smile, as she thanks each server. This only makes her that much more appealing.

Sometimes, out of anxiety, Lauren raids the refrigerator at her home and while visiting us in Newport Beach. Eating endless portions of healthy food becomes a concern to me. This only happens when she is anxious. Never purging, but binging often, is a bit of an eating disorder. On the other hand, she nourishes her body with healthy food and it is a pleasure to watch her eat. One addiction can easily transfer to another; however, one has to eat. The question is when to stop. She prefers standing in the kitchen while eating. I once suggested she sit down and stay present while enjoying her food, knowing that there is an end, but she is annoyed that I even made the suggestion. Instead of one salad bowl, she would eat three.

She munches on rabbit food, while she devours my homemade soup. Lots of veggies with white meat chicken are her favorite dishes. I always have a pot of soup simmering the minute she arrives home. The soup disappears by the next day. Sometimes I make two pots, with a whole roasted salmon. It is a pleasure to have my girl home, and watch her enjoy her favorite foods.

Cooking becomes great therapy for Lauren and she has a great style. She often invents her own recipes, never really using a cookbook. She definitely has a knack for creating new dishes, using the freshest ingredients. Tons of olive oil over grilled veggies is her staple, along with salmon or a little chicken. Garlic, onions, and peppers delight her taste buds. Missing our California fresh farmer's market makes her really want to return home. Yes, she is a foodie. Again, being sober enhances the joys of life.

Lauren always makes a home in her New York apartments. I remember her West Side apartment at sixty-ninth and Broadway. She is lucky to live across the street from Central Park and resides on the ground floor of a brownstone. It is a sublet, but nevertheless, it has her Bohemian style. A long room, connecting to a long bedroom, brings a sunny view of a woodsy patio. The yard, with a table and chair, invites her to paint during free time. That, and a cup of tea with a little classical music, set the tone for a lovely Sunday afternoon.

Going to Harper College, to master Italian, becomes stimulating along with yoga, cooking, hiking, meditating and painting, but being of service to new, troubled girls is what Lauren loves best. Later, she transfers to NYU to pursue life coaching. Our daily phone calls tell me that Lauren loves life. Only sobriety brings her to this level.

Detoxing from all poisons automatically transfers Lauren to a higher conscious level, one that I can clearly hear in her voice. She is walking on a pious plane that attracts the positive light from the universe. This is her mood stabilizer. Yes it fluctuates, but the lows are less pronounced.

Clean living and using her daily principles make her a better person, as she matures with great wisdom and knowledge. I am proud of our girl, damn proud, for she has come so far, all on her own. Her father lights up when he speaks about his girl. "The girl is a Zussman; of course she would succeed."

David brags and shows her picture to everyone at home. Lauren is a bit disturbed when she learns that Dad shows her pictures to the local waitresses and mechanics, but a dad is a dad.

David was a trader years ago and it is ironic how Lauren is attracted to this kind of man. After many superficial dates, Lauren meets Logan, a Wall Street hedge fund trader. Logan is a genius, almost savant-like, but passive and shy. Their first encounter begins at the Guggenheim Museum, when a mutual friend introduces them. Logan immediately takes a liking to Lauren and they date for a few months. Both are painters and they paint on Sundays. Logan is a graduate from John Hopkins and was a pre-med major, but switched to Wall Street. Lauren gives me a thumbnail description of the relationship, as the weeks of dating progress. "I have never met anyone so brilliant, yet he really doesn't get spirituality. What you see, is what you get, and how far can that go? Besides, he likes to party with his friends at the Hamptons during the summer. I secretly think he is a party animal and hasn't mentally graduated from his college days."

His immaturity is the kiss of death in this relationship and it is just a matter of time before the breakup. As Lauren pulls away, the relationship ends with mutual respect. However, all breakups leave you empty.

Lauren loves her women's group and her girlfriends. There is a real sisterhood that exists and blooms with each season. As spiritual as they are bright, intense conversations unite these sessions, whether they are Twelve Step based, or just a gathering of friends at her apartment.

Unfortunately, I meet many of these magnificent women at the funeral and their beautiful smiles and presence are just as I imagined them to be. They all seem like sorority sisters, but in reality they are professional, sober women who are now our children. They all have so much love and compassion for each other–authentic souls touching other authentic souls.

During Lauren's transitional time, she often dines with the girls and enjoys being single. Some have boyfriends, some are single. Regardless, they always make time for each other. This is Lauren's other family. It is a sisterhood that can't be replaced. They would converse at a bookstore, reviewing the inspiring books, or be silly, picking out the newest shade of lipstick. From laughter to tears, they are all showing up for life, and for each other.

Lauren takes a "Mama Gina" workshop in Manhattan to learn to trust and be open to love. I think it was only then, when she let her defenses down, that she became available. Soon she meets the love of her life. As she trusts herself and knows what she needs from a partner, the law of attraction brought her Alex, another man from Wall Street. It is hard for her at first to make any kind of commitment and her schedule is overbooked. They have many first dates, while getting to know each other. Almost like radar, Lauren knows that there is a spiritual attraction as well as a physical one, right from the beginning. She calls me up after dating for a couple of months.

"I think I am over my head. I am a little scared. I get butterflies in my stomach when I'm with him, especially when I see him after work, in his three piece suit, but yet our connection is magnetic."

"This doesn't sound like you." I said

"He has everything I want in a man."

On the phone my mouth is open, but I do not say anything. I am shocked, but pleasantly surprised and happy for her. For Lauren to make these revelations after a couple of months, I know this could be "the one." She then tells me, "Alex has an eclectic personality. He can be in a business mode, very serious, and the next minute he can be in the park, shirtless and sexy, playing the guitar. He can pull me in with words of wisdom, and at the same time, make my knees shake. He's the real thing."

As time goes by, the relationship grows deeper, and most importantly trust, love, and honesty prevail. Creating this lifestyle, through sobriety, brings strength. The layers of an authentic life begin to unfold. She is ready to share her life, unconditionally.

"Alex is strong, yet kind and soulful," she states. I listen carefully, without being too nosy. She cannot see my face on the phone, but I smile with delight. I know he must be one hell of a man for my daughter to fall for him. He sounds like a keeper to me. I think what Alex has that others lacked is his sensitivity and spirituality. Besides the physical attraction from the beginning, Lauren knows that he has the qualities that make this relationship a lasting one.

"Mom, Alex is spiritual and yet worldly. He is bright, sharp, yet funny and entertaining. He has kindness, warmth and honesty. Alex honors me as a woman and I trust him."

That hit the nail on the head. SHE TRUSTED HIM. Dorothy finally was surrendering to true love. I heard this clearly. Months later, Lauren tells me about their future together. "We are on the same wavelength. He gets me and I am not afraid to share, yet I want to guide him through life, as well. I am sometimes afraid, because with Alex, there is no turning back."

I am stunned for Lauren to be so candid, so honest, and so vulnerable. Plans are in the making, not only to get married, but to move back to California, after completing her degree from NYU in life coaching. A dream comes true, for all of us.

Her love and work are all that she needs, and she is on that road. Indeed, her beautiful world is establishing a new reality–a sober, wonderful life with inner peace. Lauren is a walking example of what a sober life can be: a life in progress, expanding daily.

Six weeks before her passing, she is visiting us and at the beach she states, "Mom, as good as things are, I am afraid that it can all be taken away." It has since haunted me. She not only conveys her fear of losing this good fortune, but she thinks that she isn't going to have a long life. Overlooking the Pacific Ocean, I remind her that these are old messages playing with her head. "Oh, honey, this is your old depression talking–your old tapes talking. Go for the gusto, sweetie, you deserve it."

Lauren smiles, "Mom, I'm going for the gusto," convincing me that she is, indeed, at her peak.

I took off work to spend the day with her at the Montage Spa in Laguna Beach. It was our last day together–our last, glorious day together. It felt like we were meant to be together, basking in the sun, hand in hand, on the oversized, comfy, lounge chairs, watching the waves of the Pacific Ocean, sharing our dreams.

Lauren wrote the poem "In His Arms" at the luxurious Montage Hotel in Laguna Beach. Coincidentally, she died in Alex's arms. Synchronicity was all other the place.

Alex wrote to me about Lauren's last seventy-two hours with him.

The Saturday night of Memorial Day weekend, I decided to take Lauren out for a sushi feast downtown. We met in front of the restaurant and Lauren was radiant. She was wearing a red, wrapped dress. As we had a splendid sushi platter, we laughed all the way through the meal. We loved sitting at the bar, so we could be close; a table for two usually seemed to be too distant. After the meal, we ambled through the streets of New York, arm in arm. A long walk after a great meal is what we did often.

The changes of the seasons were reminding us that summer is almost here. We turned in early that evening, chalking it up to another endearing evening. Looking forward to the weekend, we wanted to start the next day well rested.

Lauren and Alex were close friends with Sara and Mike, their happily-married friends. They were going to the New Jersey Beach, and even though it is not Newport Beach, it is the water where Lauren thrives. Alex continued:

The following morning we got up early. Your daughter so loved morning parties of just lounging about and listening to music. There was plenty of goofing around as we packed up our stuff for the beach. We got out of the house, and headed to Whole Foods for our picnic. We spent an hour wandering the aisles. I do believe Lauren would have moved into the salad bar, if she had the chance. We arrived at the beach in the late morning, and Lauren seemed so at home.

Alex's reflections continue:

I remember seeing her and Mike talking near the water, and just thinking about how much I love her. Sara asked me what I was thinking and I said that I never believed that I could fall more and more in love with someone as the time went along. I felt so grateful that day. At one point, I convinced Lauren to play paddle ball with me, and we had a good time being silly, however, she took the game seriously. I always respected how athletic she was—one of her many, many talents.

Later the foursome had a feast at Alex's house. Lauren made one of her delicious salads. They all spoke of the meaning of life and everything seemed so perfect. Lauren and Alex woke up Monday morning, Memorial Day. No work, but a jog in Central Park was planned. Alex recalls the last day.

The morning was a perfect, sunny day. I awoke to Lauren already up and we greeted each other warmly. I do know that we never took each other for granted. Each embrace was like the first one. The morning light was streaming into my place and we eagerly greeted it. The winters can be so cruel. As usual, we were dancing around like goof balls. Lauren was beaming that morning, simply radiant. Our happiness carried us into the park. I do believe that I have never seen her happier than that morning.

Alex told me that our daughter made him so happy, and that she was the most remarkable person to know and love. He knew that being in love was a unique learning experience, one to be cherished for a lifetime.

Alex planned on coming to California in August to ask Lauren's father for her hand. With both families joined on the beaches of Laguna, candles and scented red roses along the sandy shore, a romantic, formal proposal was to take place.

Due to Lauren's unexpected death, this never officially happened, but in some weird, spiritual way, they were already united. As sad as it was, she not only died in his arms, but was ecstatically happy, in love and at peace with the world.

HEIGHT: 5'8" BUST: 36 WAIST: 24 HIPS: 36 SIZE: 6 HAIR: BROWN EYES: BROWN SHOE: 9

Lauren's 21st Birthday with Oprah (2003)

Family

CHAPTER 6

The Twelve Step Program:
Bill W. and His Angels

*"To the world you may be one person,
but to one person you may be the world."*

Bill Wilson

Bill Wilson, the founder of Alcoholic Anonymous, developed the revolutionary Twelve Step program. It is the most successful program for alcoholics to stay sober. This is also a successful remedy for eating disorders, narcotics, gambling, sex addiction, and other addictions.

There are more than two million AA members in 150 countries. The Twelve Step program promotes a moral inventory, an admission of powerlessness, a commitment to service, and surrendering to God or a higher power. By helping other alcoholics, one cannot only be of service, but can also continue the flow of daily sobriety. This is the key. The beauty of this program is forming deep, meaningful friendships with people that have the common thread of alcoholism.

When Lauren hit rock bottom, after her near-death experience at Lake Havasu, she knew she was powerless over alcohol. By ignoring life's challenges and checking out with drinking, she was able to avoid all uncomfortable feelings and responsibilities. The destructive old tapes were the following:

"I deserve to drink, not follow the rules of life, and repress all feelings in order to make my body feel good through alcohol."

I asked Lauren, "What made you change your behavior?"

"Life was empty, meaningless, and dangerous. My soul and spirit faded in my everyday life. Not only was it a no-win situation, but the depression and loneliness would return."

Lauren officially joined AA after her two-week outpatient rehab program. The first year was the most painful and challenging. Not only was she eliminating all drugs and alcohol, but she had to take moral inventory of her past behavior. Lauren had to admit to all her character defects that contributed to alcoholism and self-destructive behavior. I remember her revisiting her past relationships with her family and friends to make amends with any harm she caused.

One day, while we were making soup together in the kitchen during one of her visits, I read an intense look on Lauren's face.

"Mom, I am sorry for all my negative behavior in high school. I am sorry for how I treated you, Dad and Ash."

"That was a long time ago, honey."

"I know at times I could not follow the rules of life."

"That was yesterday, today is today," I said.

"I had a lot of anger."

I melted and hugged this wide-eyed child speaking from her heart. As the days passed, Lauren continued to journal and recount the previous years. She retraced her actions and wanted to make amends with all the people she hurt. It was facing the dark ghosts within and cleaning the slate.

"Mom, I want to call Myrna and apologize for ditching her daughter when we were all together at that San Diego Hotel. You, Dad, and Nicole's parents went out and left us alone. I didn't treat Nicole very well and I want to make amends."

I asked, "What exactly did you do?"

"Mom, I ditched her in the hotel to be with another, cooler girl."

I was shocked. This happened ten years ago. It took incredible courage to face these people and ask for their forgiveness. This was her first step of going beyond her narcissism, her self-centered world.

I am so proud of her receiving her chip the first year. A chip is the celebration of sobriety and it is considered to be a birthday each year. It welcomes a prosperous and meaningful life.

Sitting among fellow AA members, as the proud mother, I feel like she has won the lottery. A beautiful, shining star takes the microphone to celebrate this day and accept her chip.

"I was a broken spirit with a lot of demons showing up at my door. Today, I take one day at a time and continue to go to daily meetings. I will continue to work with my sponsor." She continues to tell her story of sticking to the program. I start to tear up.

"I want to thank my parents, who are here today, for standing by me during this difficult time and all the friends who have welcomed me since the first day."

Now I need a Kleenex.

At the end of the meeting, we go around the room and introduce ourselves. In this circle of a hundred people, each person says their name and announces "I am an alcoholic." So when it is my husband's turn, who is not an alcoholic, he says, "Hi, My name is David and I am an alcoholic." He is lost in the camaraderie and, like a parrot, says what everyone else is saying. I thought *later* that this was hilarious. Then it is my turn. As I rise, with a sniveling, tearful, pathetic face, I announce, "In case you haven't guessed, I am the mother." It is one of my proudest moments, witnessing the beginning of a transformation of a brave, young woman who really has chutzpa.

After the meeting, David and I join Lauren with mostly older, gray-haired men for breakfast. I am exhausted with swollen eyes from weeping, but regardless, I am a proud mama. I remember Paul, a sweet, nice-looking older man who befriended Lauren from day one. Paul had the warmest blue eyes, was soft spoken, and was clearly a soulful man. They were the fatherly men that celebrated her success.

This event was the beginning of her sober journey–one of being true and honest. By discovering the little girl within, she nurtured herself to a state of clean living. Over a phone conversation Lauren said, "When I walk the streets at night, and I feel alone with sadness, I sometimes feel like I'm seven years old. I know this is the time to retreat and take care of myself."

This became her holistic life. She took one day at a time. New friendships were made, as she released old friends who drank and partied most of the time. Yes, the demons would sometimes try to invade her mind, but she always returned to the place of love–self-love. As she persevered on the street of Manhattan, I imagined her emulating Mary Tyler Moore, throwing her hat up to the sky, on Madison Avenue. The light from within was already there, getting brighter, and she started to attract positive, eclectic people from all walks of life.

Every morning, to overcome any anxiety in this new city, she would light a candle, make a pot of tea, and write to God in her journal. She wrote, "Please God, give me the strength to get through this glorious day." There were many days that she not only asked me to throw her the rope but she asked God as well.

She needed all the support she could get, but in reality, it was Dorothy with the red slippers that had more power than she had ever imagined. That and the faith in God got her through her darkest days. As the sun began to shine, the elevation of peacefulness began to set in on a regular basis. That is the true gift of sobriety. Her appreciation journal and her spirituality became stronger and stronger. Lauren called me one evening and expressed her transformation.

"Mom, I feel reborn here. I love the fresh, crisp air and the excitement of the city. Even the meetings are incredible."

"How are the meetings going?" I ask.

"I see so many people that I know from the fashion and movie industry at the meetings."

I ask, "How does that make you feel?"

"Strong and it gives me a sense of empowerment. I am among the sober alcoholics, who want to live a clean life, and I have made so many friends. We are all on the same page."

That night, I had a smile on my face from ear to ear. That was my Tootsie girl, my shining star; the girl with the biggest heart was making it on her own. Amen.

AA has millions of branches and there is always a place to attend a meeting. When Lauren was modeling in Italy, she always found a ride and a person to help her attend a meeting. Translators were also available. There are no excuses to miss meetings on a regular basis.

Even though we were not face to face, I felt the intensity in her voice as we spoke on the phone, often in the evening, after a full day of work.

"When I start skipping meetings, the obsessive thoughts begin to emerge."

"What thoughts?" I ask, as I listen to a soft, gentle voice.

"The feelings of worthlessness set in. It sets in like a brewing, dark storm. I start to go within and shut out the outside world."

"Then what happens?"

"Then I know it is time for a meeting and to reconnect. I begin to go into the danger zone of self-loathing. It is my inner tube in a dark sea of danger."

"I hear ya, sweet pea," I say.

This, of course, is tearing at my heart. However, I must let her go through this tunnel. Meetings are confirmations of one's sobriety. Lauren makes time for her meetings before anything else and it is her first priority. No one else can fix this. She has to go through it herself.

"I need to go to meetings for my daily peace of mind. It gives me the strength to get through my day, especially when I am experiencing sadness, depression, or anxiety."

I ask, "Do you want to go back into therapy?"

"No. My meetings give me the tools to survive in this world. It is my therapy."

The Twelve Step program begins the journey to a spiritual awakening. As I am having tea with Lauren one afternoon, while visiting New York, I see a light in her eyes that I have never before witnessed.

"I feel a new strength that I haven't felt before."

"I see it in your face," I say.

"I know I am going to be okay."

"I KNOW you're going to be okay."

She continues. "I realize that I have a disease–the disease of alcoholism. I know if I stick with the meetings, I can stay sober."

"You're doing it; you're handling it. I am so proud of you."

"I must do the work, the work of the Twelve Steps, and each time I interpret the steps with a new awareness–a new awakening. Sometimes I feel it is a gift from God. He is speaking to me."

I am convinced that part of her destructive drinking was to alleviate her depression, anxiety and self-loathing. Her reflection of the disease would expand to many levels, throughout the eight years.

I observe a "light bulb" moment in Lauren's eyes. "When I would drink, I felt relieved to have the darkness lifted, only to have an empty black shell return with no feelings, no drive to do anything or be anyone."

I validate her feelings, instead of denying them. "I know, honey. It must have been hell."

"And then after drinking, my self-hatred, guilt, and shame would return only to repeat this disgusting process once again. Everything would spiral out of control."

This is the beginning of her enlightened journey–a path to true discovery. The vicious cycle is broken through sobriety and a new foundation is created.

Then she puts her head on my lap and asks me to rub her back. This was something she loved to do during her visits. It gave her comfort. It gave her peace. She merely wanted to be seven again. Perhaps, she did not get enough attention when she was seven. Perhaps she was not in touch with wanting to be loved, to feel comfort. Maybe that is why each year is a new year for someone that is sober. They are reliving the childhood that wasn't there, for whatever reason.

I remember rubbing her back during asthma attacks, as a small child, but this did not happen often. Lauren was independent, unlike her sister. Ash would love to hang on to adults and show affection–very touchy and outwardly loving.

Not too long ago, Lauren told one of her best friends, Amanda, in a letter, how she loved to hug me and how our bellies would touch as adults. This of course was during her sober years. It is bittersweet to me now. Why, only as adults, did we have this closeness? Where was

I when she was little? Where was she? Did I have a jelly brain, not to notice? Did this somehow contribute to her alcoholism? In Al-Anon, there are the three C's, regarding addiction: "You didn't cause it, you can't control it, and you can't cure it," but a mother is a mother and the cord is always there.

Sometimes in the middle of the night, I would receive a phone call. If the negative tapes set in, I was there to remind her of her incredible accomplishments, the kind, gentle soul that was hiding behind the mask of depression. The phone, ear to ear, thousands of miles between us, felt like an invisible rope connecting our souls. I reminded her that this too shall pass.

There are no failures when one commits to the program, and I am so thankful for Bill W. and his angels. Lauren's sponsors were always there, and in turn she realized the true meeting of giving from the heart.

After living in the superficial world of Southern California, Lauren said, "It doesn't matter where you come from, what your social-economic status is, or what you did in your past, for we are all children of God. The past does not define the future."

She was really speaking about herself, as well as others. This was the true moment of experiencing true acceptance. This was the breakthrough moment. This was the gift of life.

After mastering the steps, and staying sober and true to the program, Lauren became an example to others. Perhaps this insidious disease came upon her to help others. While in New York, Lauren told me about mentoring. "It is exhilarating to be a sponsor to these girls. It certainly gives me a sense of identity, a true purpose to show up for life. If I can share my wisdom of sobriety with another and give them the strength and hope to stay sober, then I know my life has significant meaning."

Lauren always had faith in her sponsees–well, almost always. If they weren't ready to commit, she kindly sent them on their way, always leaving an open invitation to return. Lauren gave her blessings, in a motherly way. "If the girls are not ready to commit, they're not ready. I tell them to go back out there and party –party until you get the message that it's a dead end, a destructive journey."

Never threatening, always nurturing, she gave them the option to return, and regardless, Lauren planted the seed. She would tell them the truth. "It has to be your main priority in life, before friends, boyfriends, work, or anything else. I never wavered because I made the commitment to God and to myself. There is no copping out. You have to make the choice–the choice to dedicate your life to sobriety." We had many discussions about the excruciating pain in the beginning.

"My first year was hell without booze. I was flooded with suppressed feelings."

"I remember, sweet pea."

"I had to face the demons, the loneliness, the self-hatred, but God walked me through it."

"And that he did, but Lauren, you did it, too. You never gave up."

Knowing this and processing it only made it easier for her to relate her story to others. She would psychologically get naked with her sponsees and share from the gut.

"Mom, I tell the girls it is up to you to make the final decision. No one can do it for you and you certainly can't do it for someone else. It is a full time commitment, your commitment. You have to use your muscle and not check out."

"It sounds like your voice becomes their voices."

"Exactly."

"But you have lived it. It is not coming out of a book."

"I've lived it, slept with it, ate with it, and shit with it."

"Bravo," I said.

Speaking at meetings instantly changed a gray, cloudy day and made it a bright one. It set the tone for the day and it helped develop her personal program. Work and personal relationships on all levels would soar as she progressed with the program.

New levels of wisdom would be mastered, as her days, months and years of sobriety increased. Sharing the trials and tribulations with others was all part of the foundation to sobriety. The interaction with others brought light, not darkness; brought hope, not hopelessness; brought love, not self-hate. Again, this was a process that developed with daily meetings. It produced an unexplainable energy that resonated among their souls. All of these ingredients added to Lauren's sobriety and kept her from relapsing. It was her rope to success. In turn, she would throw the rope to those in need, and indeed she did.

Along the beaches in California, one day during a visit, Lauren told me about the gifts of alcoholism.

"Sobriety made me grow up quickly. Each new year of maturing and accepting responsibility added confidence to my core, my being."

"What do you think you all have in common?"

"Alcoholics like to take shortcuts. We don't like to follow rules. You have to face the good, the bad and the ugly of your soul. Then the light comes on and you are *empowered.*"

"How is that done?" I asked.

"You have to do the steps. When you face the music, you no longer have to face the fear that comes with that free-floating anxiety, due to suppressing the facts. You are free."

The most beautiful revelation of Lauren's sobriety is when she accepted the fact that her sobriety was only a part of the whole. She was becoming a self-assured, beautiful woman and each year became a milestone. I told her to take her disease of alcoholism, and put it in her suitcase.

"Get out there and carry **it** in your suitcase. Then go for the gusto."

This was a standard line and ongoing advice that I said often and she would repeat it back to me with each victory.

"Mom, I felt like shit today, but I put it in my suitcase and went for the gusto."

"Bravo, Toots."

Our phone conversations left us smiling with glee, as I awaited her next visit. Each time, this high-spirited fairy would enter our house from an exhausting New York flight; I knew our girl had finally arrived.

During a summer visit from New York, we found a cove in Newport Beach and made a picnic. We were side by side, soaking up the sun. The carefree child came out as she jumped the waves. The paradox of an innocent child and a wise, young woman reflected the sunlight, as I heard her laughter. The entitlement issues and instant gratification habits no longer existed. After deep discussions about her New York life and the joys of sobriety, we made a memory by taking home a rock and planting it in our backyard garden. It symbolizes the rock of courage.

∽

CHAPTER 7

Reflections of the Past: Yesteryear

"The only journey is the one within."

Rainer Maria Rilke

When I think about raising our two accomplished daughters, I have asked myself, what would I have done differently? After viewing many videos of the family events, celebrating birthdays, holidays and weekends, I don't think I would change very much. We were always a close-knit family with all the ups and downs of real life. There was simply a lot of love between all of us.

Food was always a main theme. I love to cook and present a buffet at every major event. Thanksgiving was our favorite holiday. The grandmas and grandpas brought their goodies and we would eat for hours. Seconds and thirds were common. The scent of the house, with sage and rosemary being the main guest of honor, lasted well into the evening. The cool crisp day, with orange, yellow and red floral arrangements throughout the house, complimented our table setting. Grandma Eleanor would bring her pecan, lemon, and pumpkin pies, while Grandma Janet whipped up her famous green and sour cream Jell-O mold.

Coming from a non-religious home, I studied the Jewish holidays at Stephen S. Wise Temple when the girls were infants with the converts and other non-religious Jewish wives and mothers. I was not raised with any kind of formal religion; therefore, I wanted to attend a class. I presented a perfect Friday night Shabbat dinner, prayers, candles, and flowers included. It was a nice way to bring our family together at the end of the week. However, we did not continue this ritual after several months.

A second-grade homework assignment brings mother and daughter together. Lauren has to write a book and I guide her through the theme of adventure. It is called "The Magic Elephant" and I still have it in my files. It is about two girls, oddly enough, named Michelle and Nicole (our girls' middle names), who travel to faraway lands and find magical, whimsical people and situations. It is an enchanted adventure that grows into a delightful project. We think of outlandish names and places that enhance the story, while eating freshly popped popcorn. I feel the enthusiasm in the air as we put on our thinking caps.

Sugar Pie, Rocco Pie, and Fat Cat are just some of the characters. The Crystal Palace, The Magical Kingdom and The Marble Wall are just some of the creative places we invent. Lauren illustrates colorful, graphic pictures on each page to highlight the story. Then these works of art are bound and laminated.

It becomes a feast for the eyes, and the imaginative stories are wild. We read it over and over again and Lauren is so proud of this accomplishment. It really could have been marketed and published. Wow, even Disney would have taken notice. I wish we had invented more projects like this one. We read this together just a couple of years ago, laughing and remembering the experience.

The neighborhood children are at our house, along with the other families over the weekends. The sound of sizzling barbequed burgers and hot dogs are well tended by chef Daddy David. David's hair catches on fire one Sunday afternoon, while he grills the meat, and after we extinguish the smoldering flames the girls are hysterically laughing. The pool and spa are the main attraction for all of us, as we swim, laugh, and scream with joy.

The first month we move into this huge dream house, I have terrible anxiety. I miss the old neighborhood and my friends. Being a city girl, the suburbs feel weird and isolated, especially with the dry, arid heat setting in for the hot summer. I have many out of body experiences and I try to stay stable. The girls are seven and five years old. One afternoon we go to the local drugstore. As I hold both of their hands, going up and down the aisles, I feel like we are all little children. I try to hide my nervousness, as the aisles seem to wobble in and out. I am trying to make this all work; after all, I live in paradise, right? With time, things get better and I adapt. Decorating, writing, and menu planning take up most of my time, in between carpooling.

I think David and I are a little too protective of Lauren and Ashlie. We try to shield them from emotional discomfort. All children need to experience boredom, unhappiness, frustration and disappointment. We come to their rescue, especially if it is school related.

Many years later, I returned to teaching special education, and realized how detrimental constant stimulation is and how it hinders one's development. I remember when the girls were glued to Sesame Street, Punky Brewster, Nintendo and Game Boy.

The computer explosion is also their source of entertainment. Studies have shown that excessive computer interaction can lead to later adolescence drug and alcohol abuse, due to always wanting outside stimulation. Sometimes children just need to be bored. Alone time in their rooms is healthy and should be practiced regularly. Children really need to use their imagination and invent their own play time, even if it's sorting a drawer, drawing, doodling, or just thinking. Parents feel responsible for their endless entertainment. The outside activities after school are enough to cause an emotional meltdown. Yes, we did it all.

David buys the girls two giant black and white bean bags with their names monogrammed on these bear-faced chairs. They settle in with their blankies, as they are often glued to the TV or VCR. My husband remembers playing with an empty refrigerator box in his day, or just playing outside with the neighborhood kids. I, too, remember a much simpler life, growing up during the sixties, on the quiet streets of Chicago. After dinner, we would play tag, volleyball or just play outside.

David is a great daddy, especially on the weekends. He takes them to amusement parks, shopping malls or to the movies. Ski trips come later and these are great memories.

More board games, less electronics would have been healthier. When we played Monopoly, the interaction between all of us was healthy, as the popcorn pleased the gang with good eats.

The music and movies are another negative influence. The language and behavior convey the universal message that it is okay to get wasted. Lauren is devastated when Kurt Cobain overdoses on drugs. She comes home from school shattered upon learning the news. "Mom, how would you feel if Barbra Streisand died?" I never got the connection, but apparently Mr. Cobain related a message through his music, that it was okay to get high and check out if the pain becomes too overbearing.

Looking back, I would have taken the girls to more educational, uplifting events on weekends. Going to museums, libraries, bookstores, planetariums, etc. would have been more stimulating for them to build better outside interests. We did these things periodically, but the girls were often bored.

We took Lauren to an opening at The Getty Museum and as David and I were studying a Monet, Lauren laid down on a wooden bench with her legs straight up in the air. At thirteen, I took Lauren to The Art Institute of Chicago, and she fought me tooth and nail not to view this monumental museum, only to really enjoy it after all. Later, her love for art and museums grew as she aged.

I would have delayed many materialistic purchases, or I would have had the girls earn them by doing various chores around the house. I did have a chart on the refrigerator door to be checked off as the chores were completed, but that responsibility faded as the weeks went by.

I would have liked more educational games that stimulated the mind and less mindless TV. Toys, clothes, and the hottest gym shoes were automatically bought. At times, I had wished a man with a truck would take all our televisions out of our house. Sometimes we each had a TV on, all watching a show, in a different room.

As children, the girls have many extracurricular activities. Upon waking up in the morning, my mind has to focus on what day it is. I have to think if the girls (which girl) has piano lessons, soccer practice, Brownie meetings or Hebrew School classes. Who is carpooling and what time do I pick up? How can I be at two places, at the same time, picking up each girl in a different carpool? Is it Tuesday or Wednesday? Did I switch the day with my neighbor?

Lauren has artistic talent. We should focus on that. Too many activities cause a burn-out; however, soccer is very good for her self-esteem. It seems like they are going in too many directions. No wonder we have so many kids with ADD. They are all over the place. The world is moving too fast. Sometimes, it all seems like a fast, moving dream and we are all exhausted.

Sleep away camp becomes a blast for each girl. During this time it gives David and me a chance to reunite and catch our breath. This gives the girls a time to be with nature and enjoy a healthy lifestyle. Camping, hiking, crafts and games are great experiences. Even outdoor science camp, during the school year, is an awesome way to educate our kids.

I would have volunteered more often with the girls, maybe at a soup kitchen. The girls really needed to experience being of service to others more and focus less on themselves. We did visit an old people's home during the holidays with their Brownie group, but I would have liked to practice this ritual regularly.

One November day, we drive by a homeless man near our shopping center the day after Thanksgiving and the girls suggest we go home and make a left over plate of food for him. Rolling down the window, the girls hand the goodies to this disheveled man. The bearded, dirty, sun-tanned man is incredibly grateful and smiles with missing teeth. I see delight not only in the man's eyes, but in my children as well.

The girls do have big hearts and are often thoughtful, surprising Mom with breakfast in bed. Overcooked eggs, burnt toast, and love notes are presented on a tray with a flower from the backyard.

Homemade gifts for Mother's Day are proudly presented and cherished.

Gratitude is another issue that needs to be emphasized. We did this only during Thanksgiving. I would type a note and place it on everybody's plate. This started the conversation, as others joined in. I told everyone why they are so special and why I am grateful to have them in my life. Actually, the presentation was quite lovely. I thought John Boy from *The Walton's* would soon appear and put in his two cents.

Alcohol was not overused in our house, however, we drank our wine at five o'clock, often sitting in our backyard, overlooking the orange, red and golden sunsets. This was a ritual. It is possible that our daughters equate alcohol with a sense of release, instead of reading a book or having a nice cup of tea. My husband and I are not alcoholics, but alcohol was readily available, always served at our parties and was on our dinner table. I do not think this was an issue, especially if we lived in Italy, but since my daughter has battled alcoholism I do retrace my steps. Even with a wholesome Shabbat dinner, wine was the way to celebrate.

When Lauren had her court case for possession of marijuana, we did everything to protect her from losing her driver's license. We did not want her to be unable to drive to work and school. If convicted, an automatic suspension would have occurred. Did we enable her to continue her irresponsible behavior? Later, she was in a car accident and we did not know at the time that she and her girlfriend had been drinking. Her friend was driving Lauren's car. They could have been killed or they could have killed someone. She convinced us that the uninsured foreigner was at fault, even though he was rear ended. It did a lot of damage to the car. Unfortunately, there were no consequences to keep her from repeating her mistakes.

Were we good, caring parents? Yes. Were we too permissive with our rules and discipline? Yes. This, of course, is all hindsight and it is a wake-up call for others. As an educator and advocate to parents with special education children, I emphasize discipline with love and limits. There is a thin line between helping your child and having your child step up to the plate.

Our children are always our first priority. David has a kind gentleness with both girls, and to this day, he would walk through fire for either one. He tries to tell them about the world; about life lessons; about hard work and perseverance. He has a good audience as I watch their wide eyes listen to their daddy speak in a kind voice. He gives them the power to go out there, after their dreams. He believes in both of his daughters and I think they will always have his voice within their hearts.

David would always joke with his girls, act silly and talk about farts. They would all squeal with laughter. From pumpkin cut outs, to dyeing Easter eggs, to trick-or-treat outings, he was always the third kid. The world was safe with Dad.

Good father daughter relationships give young women the power to go out there in the world and become successful. We produced fearless daughters with put away power when it came to food and they had a fire within their bellies when it came to taking on the world.

All in all, we were not perfect parents, but David and I did our best, given the tools we had. There will always be room for improvement. When our girls became young adults, we were very proud of both of them. They grew to be responsible, productive, successful, young women. What more could we ask for?

CHAPTER 8

Modeling vs. Life Coaching: A Change of Heart

"Nothing liberates our greatness like the desire to help, the desire to serve."

Marianne Williamson

Lauren continues to model for Ralph Lauren, Proenza Schouler, Jill Stuart, Ted Baker, Nautical, Danskin and J-Lo. She is the most requested fit model at Ford. Having years of experience as a print, fit, and showroom model, she is always a professional. Her knowledge of pattern work and technical design makes her that much more in demand.

Lauren makes an individual television appearance on Entertainment Tonight with Jennifer Lopez, modeling her line. She also models on E Entertainment representing a famous make-up artist. I am fortunate to view Lauren modeling a Lela Rose wedding dress and I dream that Lauren will someday repeat that breathtaking image in front of all her friends and family. Modeling gives her great opportunities, especially since she loves to travel.

However, after living in New York for a few years, Lauren starts to feel restless and searches for a new direction in life. She decides to return to school at NYU, leave the agency at the top of her career, and become a life coach. In the meantime, she takes classes and models full time. Lauren is often exhausted, yet exhilarated, with her new adventure and wants more meaningful work. As a gifted, intuitive coach and healer, Lauren wants to dedicate her life to her love of service.

Lauren tells me one night on the phone that she is ready to share one of the most important steps to sobriety: acceptance.

"Mom, I couldn't help others until I found acceptance within myself."

"What do you mean?" I ask.

"I had to let go of the past with all the mistakes I made and people I hurt."

"But you've done that, Toots. I've heard you many times talk about this."

"No, Mom, it is taking it one step further. I had to accept that *I will not always be perfect.* Acceptance is overcoming perfection."

"You mean accepting the whole enchilada?"

"Exactly. It is the road to peace: letting go of the worst, holding on to the best, moving forward with life."

"It must give you a lot of freedom, a lot of breathing space to realize this," I add.

"It is a light bulb moment. It is having forgiveness and self-acceptance which then turns into love, hope and joy. When you love yourself, you can then love others and accept their shortcomings."

Lauren is silent and then she adds, "It was the critical voice within that made me want to drink."

"Wow! You blow my mind."

"Why, Mom?"

"…because it *is* the key to truly believing in yourself and in others. It is a freedom from bondage."

"Yeah, and I finally get it. I want to spread the word to my sponsees. I want them to really get it."

102

"I'm sure you will, honey."

Lauren has the natural ability to read people's pain. From her own experiences and struggles, she can identify with the darkness of self-loathing. She can speak from her heart about not trusting others, the fear of rejection, and the avoidance of psychic pain. Lauren states, "The obsession of wanting control produces debilitating fear and inertia. You have to learn to give it up. This is one of the main reasons people turn to drugs and alcohol."

On some levels Lauren is fearless and I think it started with her father having confidence in her since playing on that soccer field. From the shortcuts she took in high school to becoming a successful young woman, it was a profound change. Only she could have done this. The Twelve Steps prepare her for overcoming many challenges, but it is her tenacity and dedication to living a healthy and honest lifestyle that brings out her best self.

This is why modeling is no longer in her cards. She has an intense dedication to taking her gift of wisdom and sharing it with others. Lauren is a beautiful, poised model with eloquent speaking skills and it will be her vessel to deliver the goods.

The classes at NYU inspire her even more and promote a new awareness to her curriculum of knowledge. Advanced psychology, human sexuality, and behavior modification are only some of these classes. Meditation and yoga classes have been ongoing classes for years. It is all part of the body, mind and spirit with the healing process. Her motivation is not to be an international model, but to be an international author and speaker on life coaching.

Lauren produces a resume to circulate after she obtains her certificate in life coaching. This is her dream, her vision and her life's purpose. The following states it clearly:

"Coaching is a multilevel support system to facilitate lasting change. The transformation begins in the mind. Our behavior begins and ends in our own thought patterns. The only way to approach change is through altering the process of thought about the issue. These changes are sustained with determination and commitment.

I am a holistic coach specializing in personal development, spiritual counseling, and lifestyle management. My focus is in integrating the body, mind and spirit. By creating momentum and focused direction, I facilitate people towards the fulfillment of their life's purpose, visions, and goals. My hope is to help individuals correctly identify their strengths and use them to increase and sustain their respective levels of happiness."

In addition, Lauren sends a letter to one of her NYU professors stating her previous work and service:

I just wanted to introduce myself and share with you a little bit about my career as a personal and holistic coach.

I have been working in fashion for the past 10 years and I am still currently working full time. About 5 years ago, I began doing volunteer work with young adults as a mentor and supportive counselor within a few different organizations. I have been coaching women continuously over the past 3 years, focusing on a holistic, healing approach dealing with personal development, with a focus on spiritually, health and wellness. We address issues such as self-esteem, fearful emotional blocks and negative thinking patterns, changing the way we think and see ourselves from within. We develop strategies to obtain personal and professional goals and new ways of thinking and behaving in the world.

Many of the girls I've worked with are between the ages of 20-35, recovering from addiction, alcohol abuse, eating disorders, low self-esteem, and depression. I have been honored to share and witness miraculous changes within these women, allowing them to completely transform their lives.

I began taking the personal life coaching program at NYU and I am so thrilled with the program, learning so much and deeply developing my skills. Please send me the list of required reading for the upcoming class, so I may prepare in advance.

Lauren wants to tackle this class during the summer and finish up with her classes by the end of the year. Alex and Lauren are going to move back to California and she will start her life coaching career. We are thrilled to have our daughter and Alex with us, and we are so proud of her wise choice of this exciting life. After years of struggling to find herself, she meets the man that connects with her spiritually, emotionally and intellectually. When it is right, it is right.

Every victory brings her joy and acceptance that contributes to her new set of friends. Her light attracts others and they too are striving to be their best. This of course includes the absence of drugs and alcohol and the people who gravitate to them. This is mandatory, as she makes this revelation: "Alcoholism, or addiction of any kind, does not predict one's future. Life can change. It is up to each individual to develop their strengths, character, wisdom, morals, and values. This does not happen overnight. I started this process in Beverly Hills and continued slaying the dragon for years. It is definitely a work in progress."

Her fears of living, of dying, of rejection, of illness, of success, of failure and even of drinking, become quiet voices that dissipate more with time. From time to time, the ebb and flow of darkness reappears, only to fade with more intensity after each episode. This is reality and quite normal.

She knows that anxiety does not last forever, and once she tackles the war zones of life, a world of joyful living evolves. This can only be accomplished by being clean and sober. Lauren's life flows and this is how she becomes an example to others. Never wavering, never failing, never quitting, her true commitment to sobriety empowers her to teach others. By walking the talk, she becomes a model for others. "If she can do it, I can do it," is what her sponsees say and aspire to do. The inspiration and zest for life is contagious. This is why her AA sisters gravitate to her, as well as all the people she meets along the way. Clerks, waitresses and waiters always remember the genuine connection they had with Lauren, and I have received many emails from so many strangers with love and gratitude for having known her.

One of her sponsees recently wrote to me:

"I just celebrated 3 years of sobriety. So much of my recovery is due to Lauren's guidance, and I pass along her wisdom to my sponsee now. Lauren is still part of the chain of recovery that serves as a lifeline for many women. None of it would have been possible if she hadn't walked up to me and told me I was in the right place and everything was going to get better. Lauren taught me that I deserve love and happiness in my life and how to walk through everything life throws at me with grace and dignity as a sober woman. I owe her my life, and

I can never express how grateful I am to Lauren. The only way I know how is to live the best life I can, pick myself up when I fall short, and to help other women get sober."

Another woman in Lauren's group was struggling with cancer and I received this letter telling me how much she helped her get through a very dark time. She writes:

"I think of your precious, darling daughter Lauren. We had lunch three times a week while I was battling colon cancer. She saved my life emotionally. I can't even begin to explain the loving manner she embraced me while I endured Chemo treatments. No words can describe how much love for her remains in my heart."

This is actually a two way street. Both women are holding the rope. As much as this poor lady received love and support from Lauren, the act of giving was just as soothing to the soul. Sponsors and sponsees come to the table with their gifts to each other. Compassion and sharing simply make us better people. What could be better for one's self-esteem than to know you are important to someone?

There are days when Lauren has to learn to shift her thought pattern by taking action. Walking on a higher plane, even when she wakes up on the wrong side of the bed, sets the tone for the darkest days, regardless of horrendous weather, long work hours or social problems. Lauren is very sensitive and there are certain days when the multi-sensory noise of the city can put her into vertigo. Coffee breaks, visiting bookstores, and attending AA meetings ease the wear and tear of the city and stress. Finding a park bench to read a spiritual book in between modeling jobs, grabbing a healthy lunch, or dropping in at the fitness center for a yoga class, are ways to renew the broken spirit. There is no substitute for hard work and this is what it takes to stay away from drugs and alcohol.

Calling a good friend just to connect, or making dinner plans with a pal can make lemonade out of lemons, as the nasty weather sets in. Remember, Lauren is a California girl and is used to perfect weather. She has SAD–Seasonal Affective Disorder–and the lack of sun only adds to her depression. Lauren has a helmet light for this reason and it does help stimulate her endorphins. She jokes about being high maintenance and the reaction of anyone seeing her in this gear.

Lauren tells me, "I can just imagine the man of my dreams, seeing me with my helmet light on my head, at five in the morning. I call that high maintenance." During a freezing winter I get a phone call from Lauren between jobs. "Mom, it is so freezing in New York that I have to slip through the revolving doors on the streets to get relief from the cold." We both have a good laugh about that, as well as visualizing the helmet gear.

Lauren has the courage to fight off the herds of elephants, even during sleepless nights. This whole process of fighting the demons does not come easy and it honestly takes years to perfect. The first couple of years of sobriety are tough, and it would be easy to go out and drink. Lauren tells me one day. "It would have been so much easier to drink–drink the anxiety and depression away, drink my life away–but I am in the fight."

Lauren becomes her creator, the soul director, the parent, and the whimsical child–whatever it takes to design the play for the day. By using her muscle, she plows through the days. Each day brings her closer to serenity, as she masters patience by using the tools of faith. She has faith in herself, faith in God and faith in the AA principles. Friends and family are always there for her, but ultimately, Lauren does it herself. It is her victory, and we hear about each one almost daily by phone. The positive energy travels between us, with deep love and respect. One day Lauren reflects on the advantage of sobriety. "It was the first step towards clarity, wisdom, peace and serenity. No one can do it for you. I had to step up to the plate and do it for myself if I wanted to live. Once you make this commitment, there is no turning back."

When I heard her say this, I knew she would stay sober. This was Lauren's mission–to master this state of being, and to be an inspiring example to others. With a strong sense of pride and incredible courage, she made it happen.

I think God picked Lauren to inspire young girls so that they can lead clean and honest lifestyles. When she spoke at our local high school, the girls listened. When she spoke to the lost teenagers at weekend retreats, she made an impact. She was the vessel–the vessel of the truth and responsibility. Speaking at AA meetings became captivating and compelling. She was one of the most requested speakers.

Lauren is a self-learner. If she reads a book that pertains to positive self-improvement, she will gather these materials for her files. We are often on the same page, at the same time, and it gives me great joy to have this connection. It honors me to be her mother. Her thirst for knowledge only heightens her self-awareness. We become soul spirits.

Life coaching will be a reflection of her writings: her knowledge of life, her academic, emotional and spiritual accumulation of precious information. Along with the concrete information, there are opportunities to meet the most interesting, wise people. These people are her sages. It is not unusual for Lauren to be sitting at a diner or a coffee house, with a group of intellectuals from Columbia or NYU, where provocative conversation circulates. Americans and foreigners, it doesn't matter, for Lauren will pick their brains, curious to know and learn from their paths, their experience, the true meaning of their lives. With a smile of delight, she absorbs the conversation like a sponge, and appreciates deeply the words of wisdom, and others gravitate to her amazing, electric energy.

Listening with total concentration to what was being said was one of Lauren's positive traits. Listening is an art in itself, and a way to dance with others. Her voice would quiet, as her eyes locked into the person's delivery. That is what made her so intriguing. She simply made you feel important. She did it well.

Lauren continued to create the internal joy of living, learning and loving. There was a whole world out there to explore, and it became her passion–a passion that could not exist without the discipline that she had to endure. Lauren learned more about the true purpose of life and living during her last eight years than most people learn in a lifetime.

ᘒ

CHAPTER 9

Lauren's Letters: An Authentic Journey

*"Italy, and the spring and first love all together
should suffice to make the gloomiest person happy."*

Bertrand Russell

The people and the places, nationally and internationally, brought new insights daily to Lauren's learning experience. The many life experiences only added to her incredible journey and her letters were phenomenal.

Along the journey of life coaching, Lauren wanted to write a book. She sent me letters, especially from Italy, and she wanted me to save her revelations for her book. I kept a file with her writings and although I can't write her book, I can now try my best to be her voice. As a mother I couldn't be more proud, as I read her words of wisdom. With all the struggling years, the battles during the teenage years, the hurricanes that would come and go, Lauren was an absolute gift.

Having a zest for life, being clean and sober and practicing a healthy, stable lifestyle brought Lauren closer to the light. This light sustained her through the daily challenges of life even when things got tough. Lauren wrote the following:

May 18, 2006
Hello Moomy,
Gosh, today was a day I definitely wanted to go home and go back into your tummy....I felt like such a little girl. I cried and thought all I want to do is to have my Moomy rub my head–and eat your soup for the soul. I need you to throw me the rope! However, before I go to bed tonight, I wanted to share my gratitude journal with you. Here are my ten for today.

1. *You, our beautiful friendship, our talks, our incredible emails, love and support.*
2. *You are so wise, so deep, and so spiritual–incredibly loving, warm and sensitive. I thank God everyday for my family. You are all my best friends.*
3. *I am grateful for my health and my body for being so strong, strong enough to hustle and sustain all this craziness.*
4. *My Italian class and enjoying such a beautiful language. Watching myself change, grow and learn; getting good grades, doing all the work and being responsible.*
5. *My friends and my family. You love me when I fall short and can't love myself all the way. You support me when I am scared and feel alone. You are always there when I go to dark places and you walk me back to the light.*
6. *Work. I work hard, and get excellent feedback from my clients. I am so grateful to be able to model and make it in NYC.*
7. *My sobriety. What a roller coaster ride, but such an incredible five years and eleven months. I have changed and grown so much and I am meeting myself as a whole woman for the first time. I love my meetings and connecting with all the wonderful friends in AA.*

8. *My medication and learning how to treat and cope with a chemical imbalance, which affects me so deeply. I am getting through it and I have a productive, wonderful life even with the challenges at hand.*
9. *Socially being able to show up for friends, functions, dates and not isolating myself. Letting people see me with all my flaws and struggles and learning that people will still love me anyway.*
10. *Spring is here. Finally the winter is over, the flowers are blooming, and the sunshine is here.*

I am so grateful for God and all the amazing blessings in my life: for the change, love and light inside me, for the love in my heart for others. I am so grateful that God gave me a second chance at life!
Amen.
I love you Moomy,
LZ JR.

Lauren's days varied with pressures and responsibilities, from dress designers' deadlines to completing assignments at NYU. Cloudy skies, rainstorms and snowstorms were enough pressure to have some funky days. Regardless of the situation, journal writing always followed these days, with a list of appreciative statements. It was easy to fall into a restful sleep with serenity and peace after writing these statements. The negative tapes were deleted, as the focus was on what she had, instead of what she didn't have. The relationship with her higher power only gave her more confidence and fearlessness the next day, as she became a reflection of this positive energy. This was the light that clearly colored her personality and drew others to her. She took this state of being with her, from place to place, only to attract others with the same magnitude of energy.

During her many trips to Italy, Lauren would draw people in like the moon reflecting light from the sun. People would pick up on her aura, and unlike most models, Lauren was very approachable to sincere people. Depending on their motives, she would clearly identify the person's persona and if no alarms went off, she would invite them in. She had more interest in listening than speaking because she wanted to absorb others' wisdom. Later, and only after she made the connection, she shared from her heart, with no pretense. False faces were not allowed, nor was small talk, and with each encounter, she took a little bit of that knowledge and tucked it away to be part of her whole.

After worrying about her international arrival on one of her many jaunts, I received a letter describing the new people and the new places that she had discovered along the way. Her sensory perception of the experiences could only be appreciated by a sober, self-aware person.

August 26, 2006
Cella Bella,

I arrived in Milan last night. It is very different in Northern Italy. Overall it is colder, more chic, more sophisticated. It is very similar to Connecticut. I have met three special people, all of which have taught me different lessons. They have opened my eyes to realizing and integrating a whole new shift in my perception of life. It was very magical with synchronicity at its base. I will share this with you—nothing, absolutely nothing happens in God's world by accident. I am witnessing God speaking to me through others and through my experiences here in Italy. I realize this is why I am here.

Through the people at work, I was invited to a beautiful home, overlooking the city with a huge terrace. Fresh flowers, a beautifully set table, and a cool breeze made it a perfect fall night. The lit candles and colorful place settings set the tone for an inviting night. There was lots of wine, traditional oil, vinegar, and incredible food throughout the evening. The hostess prepared steak, pork, and the most amazing salad. There was plenty of fine wine, pasta, cigarettes (everyone smokes) and fattening pizza. Everything I can't eat—off my list—and I felt like a freaking nun.

We sat up to the wee hours of the night, as the passion rose throughout each discussion, all in Italian. We covered music, art, theater, cinema, and history. It was truly an authentic evening.
Love,
Lorena (Lauren's name in Italian)

A few days later I received this email describing her state of elation:

August 30, 2006
Buon Giorno Mamma Z.,
   It is absolutely beautiful! I look around me and the buildings, culture, and beauty take my breath away. I keep getting misty-eyed because I can't believe my dream has come to a reality and I am here! I feel so lucky and incredibly grateful. I was exhausted when I arrived and wanted to go to the hotel to sleep it off, but I didn't want to miss a thing. I ended up sitting at a cute cafe. I was amazed at the crisp delicious veggies, freshest fish, and simplistic delicious food. The people are very nice but I must admit, my Italian is a bit rusty.
   I met a wonderful girl last night at a meeting and she is from Orange County, a few miles from our house. She moved to New York, and then to Italy to study in Florence. There was no mistake meeting this brilliant and educated woman. We connected right away—talk about there being no accidents. She took me to the Trevi Fountain and I was so taken. It literally made me pause for ten seconds. To say the least, it took my breath away. I almost thought I was having an allergic reaction to pine nuts—same kind of sensation. My eyes widened as I viewed the water, the lights, the sculptures, and the mist, all coming off from the powerful waterfall. Oh my God, Mom, I wish we could have shared it together. The little cafes, cobblestone streets, and amazing food were taken in with wonder. So many different dialects and languages were spoken, as their hands moved with passion and conviction. It is all so foreign to me. It was a completely new experience that I have never known in my life. Then we went to the fountain of Nevona again, with little sparkling lights and vines draped up the walls. It was so beautiful, Mom.
   I am off to another meeting today and hopefully some sightseeing. Here I sit in an internet cafe, listening to Italian classical music, sipping Italian coffee—very rich and strong. I am in heaven, as you can only imagine. I am taking it all in. I feel like I am in a dream. This seems so fantasy based, like I am watching a movie. I am here, and so alive and present, loving it all. I miss you, Daddy and Ash and wish we could all be here together.
I Love you.
Your Little Bambina,
Lauren

The connections that we made through her endearing letters are very special to me. A mother could not be more proud. This was not a girl but a woman, not a caterpillar but a butterfly, not an alcoholic but a sober participant of life. Without knowing it, Lauren was mastering the art of living, the road to success, because it was the process or the means that she practiced, rather than chasing the ends or a delusional state of happiness.

The state of happiness evolves only when the honest and pure principles of life are practiced, day in and day out. Healthy, honest living and attending regular meetings built the foundation to her stable lifestyle. It didn't matter what country she was in or who she was with.

With each sunrise and each sunset, her self-respect and self-love flourished. Lauren had become a whole person, and indeed she owned her personhood to the highest degree. This could not be taught. It had to be earned, by doing the work and staying true to herself.

I received another letter, quite different from the others. Lauren wanted to name it "The Art of the Heart" and mentioned that it would be a good title for her book. I added this letter to her book file.

Lauren was already an old soul; I knew this about her when she was four years old. Back then, Lauren had incredible, abstract concepts of the earth, gravity and space. She asked questions that you would not expect from a child. "Why don't we fall off the earth, when we are driving far away from home? What happens when you leave the earth? Where do you go? Why do people disappear when they get old? Do they go to outer space or fall off the earth?"

Lauren always had a fascination with the unknown, especially regarding space, time and travel. Yet, her observation of her environment, written in her letters, reflected her attraction to water.

August 31, 2006
Hey Moomy,
I just finished work after a twelve-hour day, feeling exhausted as everyone was grumpy at work. Lots of tension on site, but just remember, I am there to help.

I really love southern Italy; it is very warm—gorgeous. The weather today is like Newport Beach weather. It is pure bliss. I am staying in Naples in a gorgeous hotel, on the water. It is breathtaking and I always love the water. It always calls to my heart as it awakens me. The water makes me feel safe and free. I am a bit lonely. I have been in Naples for two days. Nobody speaks English or Italian in Naples. They speak only Napoleon. It is so weird; two completely different languages in the same country. Traveling alone is a bit sad when the views and the sights are so special. It is so moving—nobody to look over to and smile at. The moonlight is overlooking the water and all the lights tonight at dinner are gorgeous. The moonlight is glorious.

Tonight I am reading a book about the commitment to change. I was reading about abundance. I am so blessed and incredibly grateful for all that I have. I thank God many times for my family. I thank God for you and our deep connections—our admiration and respect that we have for each other. You are on my team and you take such great care of me. You and Dad are always there to listen and help me through my challenges. I love you so much. You are a wonderful mother and I appreciate all the love and support.

I am alone in this world, as I acknowledge this truth as I travel through Europe. It is funny to face this fact of life, of birth, of all the changes. I have evolved into a woman with all the chapters and phases of life. Finding love, having children and living to the fullest is what we all aim for. Yet, I know it is not forever. It is important to enjoy the moments of real living and growing. All I want in this world is to love and share life with the people I love. I want to help others. I pray to God that I find a loving, warm and kind man, who is giving of his heart and soul. I will be so committed to being the best wife and mother. I have so much to give as a woman. I have such a deep desire in my heart to give and care from my heart. We inherited this from Grandma Janet, a true queen of grace and beauty. I have thought of her many times on this trip, missing her and wishing I could talk with her. I would ask her questions. There are so many questions about life: what is important, how to cook, how to make that damn duck. How do I find peace, how to care for myself, in a loving way, as she did for others?

If only I could find a way now, to treat myself with the care, kindness and love that she would give to me. I pray that God will show me how to embrace all that I am, the good and the bad. I shared in a meeting a few weeks ago that I am just starting to see that there are different levels and facets of my personality. There are many colors in the rainbow, as there are with my identity. My ego cannot be controlled by labels, and the critic within must die. I pray for freedom from bondage to this self. I pray for freedom from fear. I pray to God to show me how to fly and be out in the real world. I pray that I can really help others. I have come this far in order to share my story with others.

I pray that God will show me how I can be useful and how I can use my gifts to help others. How can I bring someone else love, show them how to love themselves and see their beauty? I pray to God to guide me and speak to me through others, so I may be directed to be the best I can be. I pray that God teaches me and guides me, to be a good daughter, a loving and supportive friend, to be of service to any woman I can help recover, and to find happiness within. I want to be a better worker, to articulate my "art of the heart." This is what I want to share with the world. I am an artist, articulating from the soul and the heart. I am going to go for a walk. I want to stay open to what the universe has in store for me—praying for courage to go for the gusto.

I love you so much Moomy. You are my best friend forever.
Love your baby,
Lauren.

I was speechless when I read this letter. The intense drive to be her best was always her focus, as she did this out of love and commitment. I responded immediately, as she once again captured my heart.

September 1, 2006
Lauren, Tootsie Baby,
You make me cry. You are the most incredible spirit and you will find that life partner who will be the luckiest man in the world. Your inner beauty far exceeds your outer, if that is possible. Today, I was frustrated at work with all the complexity of computer data and the endless meetings, but you have taught me there are two things to remember: discipline and giving to others. It has been my main focus, as you have reminded me of that, while speaking to that incredible, sage woman in Italy.

I will be teaching seniors that are struggling to graduate to go out into the world with dignity and develop their life skills, as well as their academic ones. Our children are our Buddhas, and sometimes YOU have taught me a lot. Our give and take relationship has taught me a lot and from Grandma, to me, and to you, our family line continues to teach the essentials of life, love, giving and learning. You are my bud that has turned into a beautiful white orchid and I'm thankful for that every day.
Love,
Moomy

The "art of the heart" was really what Lauren was all about. Along the way, she had so much love for beauty, nature and the universe. She clearly tapped into a power that can't be measured on earth. Her bright light was always there to resonate with others.

Traffic, noise, bad weather and stress awaited Lauren upon returning to New York and she struggled to return to reality as she connected to the memories of a paradise setting in Italy. It was always a disappointment returning home to New York, as she stated the contrast of her environment and accepted the fact that the necessary adjustments had to be made. However, knowing what calmed the mind, delighted the spirit, and fed the soul, she could only hope to incorporate this somehow, someway, into everyday living.

September 6, 2006
Good Morning Mama,
I still feel really out of it. I ate a breakfast feast enough for five people. Ever since I have been back, I just want to recapture what I experienced in Italy, so I seem to be overeating food that doesn't come close to the amazing food I ate there. I miss the fresh olive oil. I even miss the water there–it was so delicious. I miss the fruit, especially the green figs.

I feel helpless, yet yearning to hold on to what I found there and what I felt there. The change that occurred inside me, while I was away, was a significant change in my perception of life, of people, of love, and of self. I know now what really is important. It was a beautiful twelve days of having all the layers of bullshit, distractions and meaningless obsessions fall away to the abyss. Not really realizing what was happening, but

117

just feeling lighter, I realized less is more! Simplicity was above all else and it produced purity, nothing watered down, dressed up or covered up. I appreciated pure simplicity: food, love, prayer, nature, and the connections to people. It was important to really take the time to look people in the eye.

With the change of the setting and the environment, a completely different frame of mind overcame my presence. I felt totally present, instead of distracted, every time I met a new person. I genuinely interacted with people—looked at them and witnessed their authentic character. Sometimes, I would just wonder what this man's life was like growing up, or I would be in awe of someone taking that much pride in the way they served this exquisite cheese and prosciutto.

I really enjoyed every character I met. There are lessons to learn. I loved that I just wanted to watch the show and be an observer. I had this process happen within me, not controlling the information, or examining it. I find I do this as a way of protection. Most things people say throughout the day I hear, but I don't process it or care enough to ask questions. I sometimes don't make any real connection with the random people I interact with. It is almost like the less human I am, the better and the more I will get done. Emotions just sidetrack us. The American way is to shut off the noise, the emotion, the voice and the desire in my head in order to get our asses in gear. We are always running late with eighty-five things to conquer in a day.

Sometimes I feel like a machine—the more we can produce in one day, the better. So there I took the time to really stop and smell the roses. If I were to be walking by a garden of fresh red roses—red roses so dark they almost had an eggplant hue—I would stop and smell how the sweet, bitter odor scented the air. I would grab a whole bunch of them, and feel the silky, satin petals: almost like a peach, fuzzy and soft. Then I would stop, take a look at who might have grown the roses, and where that person is. I would like to ask them a bit about themselves.

The people in Italy seem to be so proud of their contributions and creations. They all like to share with others. It was like their identity was all wrapped up in what they did and they were so very proud of it. At the same time, they really love the simple pleasure of taking their time and doing what they do.

However, one has to think, will smelling the roses pay the rent? Will society validate your hard work by maintaining the art of simplicity? I don't think so, but people don't really care. They want their roses, artificially grown, with steroids. It is about mass production, and fake perfection, chemically engineered.

As a young woman running around the big city—this big city of greatness, power, money and prestige—I feel the fear of failure and the desperation of desire. This is what triggers within my soul, during the day. The goal of integrating some of the peace and truth is to find the balance. I want to try my very best, to transition into the healthiest state of being and most of all, to take care of that little girl within. She is so confused. All she wants to do is play and just feel safe. She feels uncomfortable and tired. She needs a nap that would last three days. She wants a treat and that is where the obsession of an alcoholic mind plays in—a hungry, wild wolf, desperate to lift the feelings of loss, of sadness, of emptiness, and of loneliness. I got home and my two friends were awaiting my arrival: loneliness and depression. I feel like a reject; a failure for things I can't control. Jet lag, exhaustion and hunger resonate. I feel like a vacated building.

I met Fabio in Italy while working for Proenza Schouler and we developed a meaningful friendship. Fabio was kind, and intelligent with international wisdom. He clearly knew the human nature of people. I would sometimes struggle with my Italian and I would look into my Fabio's eyes. I would then say "Come se dice?"–how do you say?–and he would see my eagerness to learn and my innocent desire to play in the Italian fantasy world. You can't be in the play if you don't know how to sing. So I would ask Fabio to teach me to sing—to sing in different languages, something foreign. Foreign is different and refreshing. It provokes that little spirit that wants to try a new toy, a new game, be with a new friend and within that new friend (perhaps the rose gardener), discover a whole new world. The new blank canvas is fresh and naked. It carries eagerness, where dreams meet desire. The old ideas, ego, and negative tapes seem to disappear, no baggage attached and not tainted or polluted, like the same old familiar way.

In Italy, I used my senses every day. I would smell the espresso, fresh flakey croissants and every other type of Danish and delicious baked goods. I would see these chirpy, cheerful Italians begin their day with ease, ready to open shop with calmness, as opposed to us running around frantic in New York, after downing that third cup of coffee, only to run and make that damn train!

At four in the afternoon, everyone takes a nap or a siesta, or perhaps a late lunch, even though they could make twice the money if they stayed open. They seem to find their time far more important than the moola.

During the morning, I hear the city awaken slowly. The chatter and noise of movement rises, as the morning comes to life. I hear a welcoming, almost like people are welcoming each other to the day, as they offer their sincere "buon giorno".

I taste the cafe Americana, yes, set in my ways. I did not adapt to the nature of pure espresso. It just felt like it was a condensed, whole cup of coffee. Most of all, it is too quick. A couple of gulps and you are done. I love to sip my coffee, as the caffeine awakens my awareness. So I was one of those annoying Americans, asking that they make an Americano Coffee.

I feel like just being me In the morning and not worrying about hair and makeup. It is a waste of time and I'd rather get out and enjoy the life in Italy. The Italians don't really care or notice the external shit. Once again, less is more. Simplicity compliments the purity. I feel alive and awake, when I am there. I usually start the day with fresh fruit. I found myself falling in love with the figs, my favorite, because of the texture. Even the little seeds on my tongue and the thick purple skin tickled my fancy. I also loved the melon with cheese and prosciutto, and the mozzarella melts in your mouth, like it is creamy butter. If only every morning could be like this.

I FEEL YOUNG; I FEEL ALIVE; I FEEL EXCITED; I FEEL INSPIRED. I LOVE THE FREEDOM AND TIME.

Okay, I have to get into life today. I am going to try my best to just breathe and sit through all the feelings of today. I am going to pray a lot for help. I am going to try and take good care of the little girl within. She is still confused, tired and a bit sad.

I love you, Moomy. I love how you help that little girl. I know exactly how that feels over and over again in my life. No matter how good things are in life, there is a darkness that eats at you. It is a shame and a doom

about our darkness that lingers, but with love, help, medication and family, we pull out of it one day at a time…sometimes, one moment at a time. I will do my best.
Love,
Lauren

September 7, 2006
Dear Lauren,
    Your father and I are very proud of you and your tremendous growth as a thriving woman. You are experiencing life at its fullest. Life is never simple, as we trudge through the trials and tribulations. Celebrate the good and the glory. You seem to master it well. With darkness, there is always the light.
Love,
Moomy

Although Lauren could be thousands of miles away, there was a connection that we, as a family unit, always had. We welcomed her awakenings and observations, as the world expanded for her and took on new dimensions. We all rallied, as she soared with new heights and insights to what life is all about. Her celebrations were our celebrations. The next letter clearly reflects this. She was dedicated to being an example to others and sharing her gifts. Lauren's AA speaking engagements, the girls that she sponsored, and the people she guided became her weekly responsibility and passion. As the newcomers came to AA, she showed them the ropes to leading a productive, successful life.

September 21, 2006
Ciao Mama,
    Your e-mails make me cry. I am so lucky to have you as my mother. In some ways, I feel that I struggle, but then I see how God has given me the most amazing mother, friend, counselor, mentor, and a supporting loving gift. You!
    We have grown so close over the past few years and I honor you as my mother, as such a powerful, strong, selfless person. I have learned so

much from you. I could only hope to be that wonderful, when I have my babies.

I feel extremely committed to hard work these days, between school, work and meetings. I am sponsoring a few different girls, so at night I meet and speak to them, any chance I can. I am also speaking at a great meeting Sunday night. I am speaking on having a spiritual awakening, as a result of sobriety, and owning all twelve steps. I will address the importance of service and helping those who are struggling with addiction and alcoholism. I am honored that I have been asked to speak on these topics and I really plan to tie it in with some of the feelings and themes I have encountered the previous nights.

Last night, I went to a women's group. It was a great meeting with six exciting women. We all met at a cafe for dinner down in the East Village. We listened to great music as we talked about living a life of commitment to our hearts, no matter what. We all agreed to be true and loving to others, as well as ourselves. I met three new women and we went to a show. We watched this woman portray the struggles of life. It was very real. I was so grateful to be out enjoying the city, not alone, and in the company of some wonderful girls.

I have learned that desire is a gift. Many people struggle and therefore have thoughts of wishing to feel better, but having a true desire to change is a gift. Desires originate in the heart, with the intent to make a commitment. The commitment comes only after a surrender of old beliefs. I can only truly move forward and achieve a truly different result if I first surrender to the old tapes, old patterns and old thinking. Habits can be learned and unlearned.

I must let go of my mental obsessions and truly let go of reservations and the fantasy of a life with Michael. I have deep pain in my heart and a sense of emptiness. I have to face my fear of a state of nothingness, a lost love and a lost fantasy. This is keeping me from moving forward and opening the door to someone new. This emptiness is why I drank for years and it is what I still struggle with. This distraction from being truly intimate with ourselves keeps us from being happy. If I truly let go of Michael, then I have to face being alone. So much of my drinking and alcoholism had to do with running away, not from the world, but from myself. Addiction is the compulsion and obsession to put anything between me and my internal self, who had so much sadness and pain. It somehow feels that the pain of battling addiction is less painful than the pain of facing our demons.

I pray with all my heart for God to show me the way to surrender these mental blocks, negative tapes, obsessions and mostly this feeling of low self-esteem. I want to make a conscious commitment to change, to take on different thinking, which will result in different choices and, in turn, a different reality. The definition of insanity is doing the same thing over and over again and expecting a different result. So, in order to change, I need to be completely willing to let go—to surrender.

This brings me to the second theme I am going through...DESIRE IS NOTHING WITHOUT COMMITMENT TO A DIFFERENT ACTION. If I want to feel different, I must take a different action.

I know I must start with organization in order to lead a clean life. I need to clean, organize, study, and take care of myself; then I will feel good about myself. I must take on esteem-enhancing acts in order to feel I am enough. It is okay to be with myself, which ties in earlier to what I wrote about being intimate with myself.

At the end of the day, I need to look at what I have done. Did I care for myself nicely? Did I clean my apartment, make a nutritious breakfast, and organize my thoughts and schedule? Did I study and prepare for my classes, go to a meeting, try to be of service to someone throughout the day? Did I take on the outside world and choose to be with others after work? So much of my pattern is to isolate and not let people see me struggle. I cannot be truly in life unless I show up to be with the rest of the world. This is my different action—to show up for others and let it be imperfect. I don't want to experience life alone anymore and I think part of my sadness is a feeling of loneliness that is so deep and penetrating.

I live alone, sometimes work alone, travel alone for work and often eat lunch and dinner alone. I don't want to live life alone.

I had so much fun when Fabio came in from Italy and dined with me in the city. He is such a good friend and conversationalist. This city is filled with so much great nightlife and restaurants. I pray to show up to enjoy it. To truly live the life I want I will try harder and harder to be my best for God, for others, and for myself.

I love you Moomy, so much. You are always in my heart and I am so grateful for you!
Love,
Tootsie

Lauren always shared from the deepest part of her heart. If we threw her a rope, she in turn threw it to others in need. Sharing the wealth of encouragement, love, and hope always came in handy. Ultimately, self-love and self-acceptance were the objectives, and Lauren certainly mastered these during her last few years. She clearly identified the steps to lead her best life and then she followed through. Indeed, she did.

Lauren moved away from religion, prior to sobriety. She then opened her heart and returned to God through the Twelve Steps. It was her foundation to her recovery. One can believe in a higher power, not necessarily God, and still benefit from the Twelve Steps. God can be nature, science and physics. The program is still effective and it also gives one a sense of community, which is a major component to organized religion. Lauren found her spiritual and religious connection to be enlightening and it gave her an anchor to the madness of life. Going to other religious functions, with friends of other faith, was something that Lauren enjoyed doing. It was all good and it attracted the light. It only heightened her experience to connect and honor God. It is what surrendering is all about. By giving the power over to God, it began the process, from ground zero, to create a sober, successful, meaningful, and productive life. The past mistakes and lifestyle dissipated, as new and positive behavior evolved. This in itself became a new beginning.

Lauren's appreciation for history was written in a very moving letter as she reflected on her own personal history, growing up and cherishing the past. This letter was written during the Jewish New Year of Rosh Hashanah.

September 23, 2006
Dear Mom and Dad,
I want to share with you my incredible experience today. I went to services this morning at the most incredible Temple down in the East

Village. It happens to be the oldest temple in New York. The outside isn't much, but the inside was special. I sat in my seat with my dear friend, Aviva. The band started to play directly in my view. It consisted of these famous Latin brothers. Two played the violin and one played the acoustics. A woman sang with all of her heart and soul as classical music played in the background. It melted my heart as I closed my eyes and became laced with warmth. The essence of the morning nurtured my soul. I couldn't help the tears streaming down my face because it was my first time being at a service in years. For whatever reason, I had turned away from my religion. I knew it was something I would eventually return to, but I gave myself the freedom to go and explore other things, with less conformity. I think you would say "less dogmatic." I felt the Jewish faith was not clicking for me. Something about it felt dry; the history was boring and it never really struck home for me.

The Twelve Steps have brought me closer to God than I ever knew growing up. The program gave me the freedom and encouragement to develop and build a safe truth within me. I now know what my higher power truly is and throughout my sobriety, I have cried out to God starving for relief, comfort and assistance. I have shared with God my many feelings and at times I have been so resentful for the feelings of emptiness and loneliness. In reality, I finally realized that the desire for God is greater than anything in the material or physical world. The way to connect to God is to connect with others, for we are all one.

That emptiness in my soul would be the catalyst to bring me closer to others and it brought me out of myself. I finally began going to meetings more regularly and once in a while, I would feel the love of God. After learning to love myself, I slowly awakened out of my shell.

In early recovery, particularly after my grandmother passed, I went so inward and felt my heart cave in. I was just too raw and too weak to be out trying to be normal. My nineteen-year-old body had to be perfect and keep my mask on in L.A. At the same time, I had to try to keep the house of cards from falling.

This last year has been a different chapter. There has been a definite rebirth with my spirit. I feel lighter, younger and free of bondage. I started to welcome more love, more life and more light. I found my melody.

It is now so wonderful to be present with my family. For years I was all over the place, never unpacking my suitcase, physically and mentally. Finally I landed the plane, as I felt safe. My Newport Beach home became my oasis while visiting, as I also made many friends on the West Coast. The time spent with my family took on a completely different experience and the relationship with my parents became a celebration of companionship. I experience rich, simple pleasures, the best stuff on earth: the beach, the food, the laughs, the silliness, the jokes, the nicknames and the stories.

Recently, you and I started to go through our family pictures and I began to revisit my past. Before the days of the rebellion and chaos, I felt my innocence as I would get in bed with you over some hot tea and a stack of pictures. We took a trip back to our roots and for the first time since Grandma's passing, we were able to look at pictures of her. Grandma's eyes reflect compassion. Her soft, brown eyes invite you to get comfy, put your feet up, lay back and let someone completely nurture and take care of you. Her patience was infinite. Her kindness and generosity were of a selfless nature, never known before to me–unconditional love.

I sat in Temple and revisited the sounds of the congregation, singing with intention. In spite of the New York rat race, the families gathered together to honor God and their faith.

The Rabbi delivered a solid, historic, educational sermon that brought back my childhood memories. That little girl within joined my twenty-four-year old body. I found myself speaking and singing the words in Hebrew—everything I learned in Hebrew school and at summer camp. The words were the same, but took on a whole different meaning. My spirit shifted as I read the words with a new pair of imaginary glasses. I was inspired to a new and higher level that was embedded in my soul. I now understand the promise of faith. I looked up at the arches and they were glazed with a gold accent. The warmth of the coral stone complimented the rustic outlines of the walls and ceiling. As the Rabbi brought the Torah around, I jumped up and kissed it and felt my faith and tradition in action. I know that God is eternal and God is one.

The New Year speaks quietly to that terrified little girl, riddled with demons. My mind and old tapes were painted with entitlement and the stubborn fixed ideas, as I would fight myself, having to pay the dues of being human. Can't I skip the work and take the class for credit or no credit? I always dodged the narrow paths and yearned for the exemption of pain and discomfort of the human experience. I would do just about anything to dodge responsibility of any sort, driven by the desperation of a dying spirit. I sucked the cash and prizes out of life. I lusted after my greed for power and wanted to run with all my treasures that were shoplifted from the store of rewards.

As I reflected on my past, I asked, "Who was that girl?" I don't know her and I can't ever accept that in this lifetime, we shared the same body. Why was she able to take my life hostage with the insanity of alcoholism? Who the hell let her in and how did she persuade the innocence to abandon the ship? I manifested a rebellious, angry girl in too much pain to endure reality.

My soul knew that it would arise from the darkness. It was the old soul of God within me. Why was she so quiet and inactive? Why did she not petition the disease? Because she knew the volcanic eruption of my big self would arrive in harmony one day and find love and reconciliation with my past. She knew the experiences that would lie ahead would make me into the woman God intended me to be.

My personal dream is to take my life, my struggles, my pain, my experience of sobriety and spiritual awakening to those who fight for their lives with the desperation only the dying and suffering could evoke. My personal dream is to live in love, to sing my song. I want to embrace, accept and love the woman I am today. I have been gifted with the commitment to follow my truth. I pray that the light within me walks each and every day with a little more love, and a little less fear.

The New Year represents the fall. It is a new cycle; like the first day of school entering second grade—the crisp air and the desire to get all A's, to be a "good girl." Then my inability to conform would set in, even with my best intentions. My irrational impulses would run wild. I wanted to be older. I saw a vision of freedom from my bondage of insecurities.

The dark winter months made me yearn for spring. The lack of light and the coldness of the wind fade my spirit. Even at twelve or thirteen, I felt like an old tired lady during the winter months. Spring sparks a new light that continues into summer. Summer nights have always felt magical to me, particularly in New York. I love walking up 3rd Avenue with

my favorite companion into the wee hours of the night, flying high with euphoria and joy. I know that living in God is the same as loving myself and loving others.
Love,
Lorena

Lauren's zest for life, going for the gusto and attracting the light within, only came upon her after years of hard work. This transformation drew people to her like a magnet. By studying life's true principles, both in and out of AA, she discovered a world that worked for her and she became a mentor to many. Perhaps she was chosen to conquer her demons, her challenges, her fears, in order to tell her story to others. I only wish that she did not have to suffer like she did in the earlier days. The pain was real, but unwarranted, especially during her teenage years. I regret that I could not have helped her more effectively. I regret that therapy was not particularly successful. I regret that we did not have the bond to overcome the jigsaw puzzles of life. I regret that we were not able to mend our tumultuous relationship, prior to sobriety. However, she would not be the person that she was, had she not lived her journey. Neither would I.

Real fears appear from time to time, for everyone. Certainly, sober people do not have it any easier and can have more challenges in life. The old tapes may threaten their state of well-being and this can happen even during a tremendous growth period. Lauren would sometimes, not often, have sleepless nights and the dark voices would settle in. Lauren told me, "It is the obsessions and compulsions of the alcoholic mind that darken the world. This is the time to reunite and share at meetings with my AA sisters." Sharing with her girlfriends was the best therapy and not only interrupted the negative tapes, but gave her a new and refreshing outlook of life. God bless Bill W. and all his angels. It is a safe place to go and work through the demons.

Despite hard work and growth, the return to conflict with the self or the world could arise at any time. Lauren wrote:

"Anything can trigger a thought or an uninvited memory. It can haunt the soul for hours. However, it is what we do to help ourselves that will bring us back to a comfortable state of being. Validation of these thoughts and feelings can be helpful, in order to release their power within the mind. Often journaling can help release these feelings or sharing at a meeting can shift our world back to normalcy."

Lauren would openly share her experiences and how she overcame the suffering, but only years later. Again, it was partaking in the necessary work to rise above the darkness of pain, as she so clearly stated in her letter:

October 12, 2006
Dear Moomy,

I heard some sad news tonight. My friend's brother was killed in a car crash, due to drugs and alcohol. I felt the wind knocked out of me. It is a familiar feeling of defeat with each incident—the friends I know that didn't make it. It symbolizes those souls who just couldn't beat it. They were constantly at war with something, after seeking treatment, coming to find it is deeply rooted in pain, avoidance, depression, anxiety, fearful obsessions, compulsions—all of these overwhelmingly powerful feelings, yet they are still distractions from facing the truth. I think what lies underneath the alcohol, food and drug addictions is the inability to be with yourself, to live in your body, to feel your feelings, to have love or compassion for yourself. I identify with these poor souls and how hard it is not to be in the world, but to be in your head—to be intimate with your darkness and your light—to embrace all colors and all the feelings. So much of my addiction was my inability to be consistently present and sit with my feelings. I think I operate on a very high frequency of emotions and sometimes it is just too much, too much to stay in the game. The feeling is desperation to be set free, to breathe, to rest even if only for a few moments. I remember what it was like. It is not a weakness, but there is a choice.

I feel so grateful I made it. I just pray that God continues to use me, to share my experiences and my strengths, to be able to beat it. I want to live a real life and have love in my life—to be able to make peace within myself and find my greatest light, most of all, so I may shine for others and give of what I have within me, for I know there is a great capacity for love and knowledge of my sobriety by cleaning out these deep holes.

Now the holes have been filled up with a solid, deep, reliable foundation. It is a foundation strong enough to hold a real house to live on. I sometimes have a hard time accepting that I have been gifted with life. I still am sometimes convinced that I am not going to make it in this life, but the evidence shows completely the opposite. Reality shows I am soaring like never before, but my delusional, skewed feelings trick me and the feelings spiral into old patterns of thinking. Therefore, the behavior, less the drugs and alcohol, continues the bondage to self-centered fears.

I am so grateful, for all of that has been dying away with every time I see myself rise above the occasion. I then experience a greater freedom and a new vision. Only God can see my true potential, for sometimes I don't even know how high and how great I can actually be. My challenge, at times, is to see it in myself and then trust that if I persevere, it will manifest as a powerful voice within—a powerful instrument of God to sing through my soul, to reach others.

Sometimes I feel so scared—scared of losing control and ultimately dying, which is the ultimate loss of control. The innocent little girl is not ready to face a truth tonight. I wanted to run back to my mommy's nurturing and protective, warm bed. I want your affection, but I am a woman who has to accept responsibility, to be a strong woman that can be present for real life—no more running away.

I pray to God to give me the courage, truth and trust to feel my feelings fearlessly, for what they are. I want to honor them, feel them, express them and then let them go, so I can remain present and of use to others. I am so drained. It is almost midnight and I have a couple of great long days ahead of me. I love life and I really love my life. I have been given many gifts, but it is my responsibility to show up for these gifts, and also believe that I deserve them.

I love you so much. You are the most amazing spiritual companion, mother and friend.

Thank you for believing in me always.

Love,
Lauren

No matter how many steps we take to maturity, we can sometimes feel like we are seven years old during times of stress. I gave

Lauren three pointers in life, ones that have worked for me and my students.

1. When life gets hard, use your muscle. There is no substitute for hard work. Each time you use your muscle, you will become stronger, thus, your self-esteem will soar.

2. When life throws you one of your three friends, (as Lauren has named them: loneliness, depression and anxiety) put each one, as they come, in your suitcase. Then you can do anything, go anywhere, and carry your suitcase.

3. Most importantly, go for the gusto and enjoy life. Don't be afraid to be happy. When you see a sunset, an ocean, a garden and you feel joy, jump on it!

I think Lauren had mastered these skills; she just didn't know it. Like the wizard telling Dorothy she had the answer all the time, Lauren discovered her own strengths, her own tenacity and her own perseverance to take on the real world of life. The next letter clearly states a revelation of the transformation. After Lauren's relationship with Michael ended she wrote:

March 7, 2007
Dear Moomy,

I have been doing a lot of reflecting recently about life and what lies before me. There has been a perplexity and a sense of being torn in different directions. I have found myself a bit confused, but fortunately I have been lucky to have support and guidance through this time. I wanted to share with you part of my process of where I am at in my life.

I have learned so much about myself in the past year. Going back to school has been incredibly rewarding–tough at times, but has really brought me to the next level of growth, in many ways. I have learned so much. I have met parts of myself I had never known. I have learned that I have a lot of drive, dedication and commitment to what lies before me, and what I have walked through. I am finally being able to develop a stronger sense of wholeness within me as a woman—a finding and discovering of wholeness and a sense of self without the validation of externals (others and society, people, places and things). I have found this through character and from within my heart to know that I am beautiful inside. I have learned and found that I have many things to offer, to share and help women in need of love, comfort and support.

I want to express how much you have affected me in countless ways. I know that over the years, as my relationship with you has healed and strengthened, it has deeply affected me and has made me feel an incredible amount of self-esteem; truly you have shown me the way to correcting these negative tapes that have riddled me all my life. You have guided me to optimum health of my body, mind and spirit. You have listened to my cries from deep within my seven-year-old little girl's heart. You have been supportive and compassionate constantly. You have listened to my everyday problems and you have always been there to help me see the truth. You've encouraged me to be kind and loving to myself. You have encouraged me to act like a woman, with dignity and respect. The support you have given me has given me the clarity and motivation to set healthy boundaries with my relationships, honor my feelings, show my vulnerability and choose the men to be involved with.

The relationship with Michael was such a growing experience filled with joy, love and healing. I think the love that I was able to experience with him, while we were in love, was incredibly healing and filled my heart in a way that taught me so much about what the most important thing in this world is—the amazing inspiration that comes from being in love.

I have experienced the human experience of truly connecting intimately with another on so many different levels. I have learned so much from the past four years from when he entered my life—all the pain, sadness, and feelings I never felt before in my life—and as I walked through these feelings, I had to really face myself and my own demons. Love can bring out the best and worst in people. It can also, for the first time, show you how to love and care for someone else's feelings and well being, sometimes more than your own. Love can be truly selfless. I had trouble at times, defining the line between selfless love and losing my sense of self.

Again, many of the lessons I have learned have been extremely painful, but have brought me exactly where I am today. I really honor and feel proud that I have made the decision to walk away. I was mesmerized and lured by the charms of prestigious living, yachts, private jets, amazing vacations, the most incredible food, restaurants, cruises, first class tickets to concerts, plays, and all the entertainment. It is the American dream— the life that shows you that you are enough in this world.

On an internal level, I felt beautiful for the first time as a woman when I was with him. It was the first time I was intimate with a man emotionally and physically. I met myself as a woman for the first time that year—who is that woman within me emerging? I secretly observed an evolution of growing into a woman. I began to think of how I wanted to care for him, nurture him, etc. I was changing before my hungry heart, before my soul. I realized that these qualities were biologically and mentally that of a new woman. This evolution and development was the beginning of a healing process. Wholeness was born in my personhood, as well as my soul.

I think the loss and grief I experienced of letting go of my first and only love was incredibly painful to process. I had never sat through the rainbow of feelings before. Even when we lost Grandma, I wasn't able to go through the human experience of pain, mourning, grieving, sadness and darkness. I got stuck in denial along the way, as if it was quicksand. At nineteen years old and only one year sober, I felt truly paralyzed and devastated. I think the loss of Michael, the loss of love and the connection with another, activated and brought back the existing feelings and emotions that were never processed.

I think part of my current bouts of depression and anxiety that have occurred within the last few years has been mainly chemical, but truly, it was also an overload of feelings and emotions. I have carried a theme of tightness and restriction throughout my sobriety that has been symbolic of my desperation to control my feelings. I think part of walking through addiction to alcohol and drugs has been a continuous challenge to go through the human experience. Much of the disease of alcoholism has to do with the inability to stay in reality. They call this "checking out." Accepting the gray areas of life threatens the soul and is terribly unsatisfying.

I have a hunger within me for extremes and a desperation for more of everything that will make me feel better and fuller inside. I think the universal and common thread in every alcoholic or addict is desperation in order to fill up a gaping hole from within the self. The extremes of love, self-esteem and insecurities fuel the disease. I think the success of

133

my recovery throughout the past seven years has been attributed to a combination of many things.

I have had a mental and psychological transformation. The way the brain processes information from daily life takes on a reprogramming of ideas and thoughts. This creates new actions. My thoughts provoke my feelings and my feelings provoke my actions, therefore, my actions shape and define many aspects of my life. The actions we take each and every day define who we are in this world.

I have gone through a complete transformation of character. I have grown to exude a grace, integrity, and humility I never knew before. I have committed myself to countless hours of self-exposure, self-discovery and honesty that I was never able to take responsibility or accountability for. I had to look at the exact nature of my being on every level—the good, the bad and the ugly. I had to face myself in the mirror of life for the first time and boy, was it tough at times. Facing ourselves is one of the bravest and most rewarding things a person can do. I have had an incredible dedication and willingness to consistently take actions when I feel uncomfortable. I will trust my intuition. The payoff and rewards are beyond measure. I have evolved to the woman that I have grown to love and honor.

A physical detox, transformation and years are needed to heal from the abuse of the body that comes from addictive and excessive behaviors. Even though I only drank and used for about four years, the body takes up to seven years to rid some of the toxins, metals, damage and cell growth. Changing the way I eat is so important.

Especially life-changing has been facing and successfully treating a severe chemical imbalance of my depression. You and I have taken the change of mind to not label it. You and Dad have seen me constantly and consistently suffer from depression. It has been one of the biggest components to my struggles since I was a teen. Walking through sobriety and learning how to live as a sober woman who struggles with depression had been incredibly challenging at times. Because of the way you and Dad have loved, supported and cared for me constantly, I have grown tremendously throughout the seven years and learned to detach myself from it most of the time. Wow, what a gift! At one point it completely consumed me, and now I have learned to, as you say, "carry it in my suitcase" and "use my muscles."

My three friends of loneliness, depression and anxiety are always lingering, but for the most part, they are sleeping. They are out of sight, out of the way of having a healthy and harmonious life. I am thrilled to say that most of my struggles that I currently go through are that of a woman going through human evolutions and growth of a woman walking through her twenties. Hormones, growing up, and becoming an adult are tough for every woman. Thank God I have you and Dad to support me through this human experience.

Lastly is the way I have grown spiritually. It has been the biggest gift of sobriety to develop a relationship and partnership with God. God has become a higher power to evoke within me to be my highest self. God has graced me with a freedom from bondage. God has carried me from myself. God has unleashed me from the darkness that weighs and burdens my soul. God has disencumbered me. God has led me to peel many layers away of pain and burden. God has led me to shed the weight of shame and guilt that has separated me from my own humanity. God has brought me to empower myself. I always wanted to get to be who I thought I should be. I was trying to be someone else, as I ran from myself for years. I know God graced me with the truth, and many times in my spiritual journey I wanted to turn into what I thought would make me "good or "happy." I know my true happiness has been attributed to the discovery of who I truly am inside. The girl with the biggest heart is something I am blessed with from the beginning of my life, and this comes from you. You and Daddy created me. God has blossomed me and carried me to grow. Many aspects of me began as a mustard seed, and through my life, I have been guided and blessed to become my highest self.

I thank both of you from the bottom of my heart. I love you with every part of my being. Thank you for believing in me! Thank you for loving me. It is the most powerful and incredible gift anyone could ever receive in life.

With that love, I have been completed. I am now able to give and share that love with someone else. I have so much in my heart. I am finally able to let go and go for the gusto!

I love you,

Toots

On May 10th, 2008, I received a lovely Mother's Day card with a heartfelt, written dedication honoring me as Lauren's mother. Simultaneously, I received a phone message, with a similar message, that I listen to weekly. Three multicolored bracelets would be arriving in the mail. I replied by sending her an e-mail.

Dear Toots,

Thank for the lovely message. Just so you know, you are my gift for Mother's Day and every day. Your soulfulness and perspective on life tells me that you are certainly on your way. You will be a gift to many. I miss you and your laughter. I would like to just sit with you at the water. Soon. Love you,
Moomy

I was picked to be this girl's mother. Through thick and thin, it had been a continuous cycle of love, for both of us.

∽

CHAPTER 10

Our Letters: Souls Meeting Souls

"Ultimately love is everything."

M. Scott Peck

David is the warm and entertaining Dad that everyone wants for a father. He loves his girls dearly and was always there for Ash and Lauren. Whether it was a fall on the playground or a skinned knee, David was there with Band-Aids and maybe an ice-cream cone to follow. But the true medicine was the love and comfort that David provided for each of his girls, always there from his heart and soul.

At Lauren's Bat Mitzvah, David gave a heartfelt speech to encourage his daughter to go out there and be the best she could be. During the speech, after a long pause, people in the audience actually thought he was becoming ill, when in reality, he was so choked up and teary-eyed, he could barely speak. His little girl was becoming a young woman and with all her accomplishments, he saw his bud blossom into this woman. It was too much for the people who, along with the family members, bawled their eyes out.

David and I met Lauren in Chicago when she first moved to New York. We had some business to attend to and we met some of our friends during one sultry summer night. We all decided to go to a bar on Rush Street, a popular spot for the young people. We were all dancing like fools and sure enough, I spotted this cute young man, and struck up a conversation about Chicago. After a short while, I pulled Lauren into the conversation and before we knew it, a fast two-in-the-morning hour was approaching.

As we were saying goodbye, this nice gentleman convinced David and I to let him take our daughter to another local bar. Our hotel and this bar were very close by. We agreed because we really liked this man and we felt that Lauren was in good hands. I saw my husband put his arm around this innocent man and then I heard him say, "Listen, I want you and my daughter to have a good time, but if you hurt her in any way, I will have men find you and you will be buried in the Nevada desert—but I really want you to have a good time." Neither Lauren nor I thought this was very funny at the time. However, we had a good laugh about this for many months.

David gave Lauren the nickname "Yorkie" since she had moved to New York and then he also gave her the name "Poo Poo." He called all of us "Poo Poo," affectionately. We don't know why, but we all laughed. The man could do just about anything and the girls would think he was hilarious.

David was very proud of Lauren's eight years of sobriety, traveling to Italy alone, and becoming a business woman. He had a grin on his face when he heard her negotiate her modeling contract with Ford. From her perseverance as a young girl playing soccer to managing a single lifestyle in New York, he found her to be amazing. She was truly the apple of his eye, as was Ashlie, and I think one of the reasons she became so successful in all areas of her life was because she had the best man to root for her. David never wanted her to fail and he gave her his blessings, always there for a heart-to-heart talk. I can honestly say he didn't miss a step in being an incredible father.

In her letters, Lauren would tell her father how much she loved him and that he was her hero. There has never been a closer father-daughter relationship and because of this strength, Lauren never wavered and would not quit. She was, in Daddy's words, "a true Zussman."

On one of Lauren's last trips home, the two of them went on a two mile nature walk, a ritual they often enjoyed. They would talk about world events, love, and the true meaning of life. Her father was a giant in Lauren's eyes, and she in turn was not his princess, but was perceived as a respected, bright, hard-working young woman. Her attributes were the real focus, rather than her beauty. Mutual respect bounced between them as they walked the streets and beaches of Newport.

It was a healthy time when Alex, her beloved, was entering that room of love and admiration. Only these two men could share Lauren's trust. The fact that she had dinner with them both in New York just weeks before her passing was another completion of her journey. Lauren was with her bookends. Her past and future were right there. I spoke to Alex by phone that night and apologized for not being able to pull away from work.

"You are missed, Mrs. Zussman. I am hearing about all the family antics," Alex said.

"Ouch," I said. We both chuckled. "I look forward to meeting you in August. The summer is a great time to visit Newport Beach," I added.

"I can't wait," said Alex.

"We will have to party hard when you get here."

"I wouldn't have it any other way," he cleverly responded. (He has a cute sense of humor, too.)

The two men, who she most respected, broke bread together. Synchronicity certainly does exist.

Ash was the little sister. She became quite an outstanding woman before our eyes. Lauren was so proud of her and was in awe of her transformation. Ash recently graduated from college and entered the field of advertising with great recognition. Lauren missed Ash more and more as the girls became older. They had a bond that could not be broken. Even with their differences as siblings growing up, they had a loving relationship.

A couple of years ago, the girls went to Florida to take on the town during a vacation. They decided to raise a little Hell with single young men in South Beach. There was a group of young doctors staying at their hotel. Ash was on the beach and got stung by a stingray. It was incredibly painful and she could not walk. Being a couple of blocks away from their hotel, Ash called Lauren about her dilemma. As Lauren tried to find one of these doctors, Ash found a lifeguard who carried her back to the pool of their hotel. As Lauren came running with a couple of doctors to rescue her injured sister, there sat Ash with the lifeguard, on her third margarita, having the time of her life.

A few days later, while the girls were sunbathing at the pool, a man with a French accent offered to give Lauren a complimentary foot massage, courtesy of the hotel. Ash was skeptical and sure enough, moments after the massage, a security officer escorted this vagabond off the premises.

After this trip, the girls became even closer, as they were now young, adult women, with great admiration for each other. Ash had visited Lauren in New York and met all of Lauren's friends. Lauren was so proud to introduce Ash to her close girlfriends. They ran around New York, seeing the sights, dining at the restaurants, and a good time was had by all.

Our endless videos and pictures, throughout the years, depicted an all-American California family growing up. Those images and a little bit of the Marx brothers' escapades would clearly show our life of joy, love and shenanigans.

Ash always looked up to her sister and wrote a letter for a college assignment that not only honored her sister then, but it still applies to her feelings for her today, maybe more so now than ever.

Someone to Look Up To

I consider a role model to be someone who can help me become a better person. My sister, Lauren, has taught me many things in life that have formed me into the person I am today. She has taught me to never have regrets, not let things block my dreams, and appreciate what I have. Watching my sister take advantage of every opportunity in life and succeed while doing so has inspired me to try new things. From her, I have learned that taking opportunities in life leads to amazing experiences in life.

My sister has had so many obstacles block her path and has found some way to conquer them. I have never seen her give up on anything in life, no matter how impossible it is. Not only has she never given up, but she has eventually achieved what she was aiming for. This has taught me to set goals in life and not let anything stop me from getting to them. I will never forget the day at my high school graduation when she walked up to me, placed her hands around mine and said, "Ash, you did it! No matter how aggravating it was, or how many times you felt like giving up, you never let go and finally graduated. From here on, you can set and achieve higher goals." Hearing this made me realize I can do anything I set my mind to.

Lauren constantly tells my family and me how grateful she is to have us in her life. She makes us feel important in her life and lets us know when we do something to make her feel great. Seeing this positive attitude makes me realize how lucky I am to have her for a sister. She often tells me how much I mean to her.

Seeing my sister's positive attitude has helped me believe I can be what I want to be and do what I want to do in life. Lauren has made me become a better person. She has taught me to find out who I am, love who I am, and still grow to be my best.

As a special education teacher, I had my students reflect on Rainer Maria Rilke's eight steps to a successful poetic life. It was written up in the *Los Angeles Times - Daily Pilot* newspaper. Lauren was so proud of this accomplishment. She wrote a Mother's Day letter, one that I will cherish for life. It was our last Mother Day's celebration.

May 10, 2008 (Mother's Day)
Dear Moomy,

I am so happy about your great news! It is the biggest gift as we celebrate Mother's Day, and you are incredible. I am celebrating you all weekend, lighting a candle for you, sending you so much love. You are in my prayers of gratitude for your health and happiness.

I am so proud of you with what you have done for these kids—changing their entire lives by helping them develop a sense of positive identity and self-worth. The affirmation of their abilities instead of their disabilities is a gift that will dramatically change their paths as they transition into being young adults. The most powerful shift is that deep shift within—a change of their perception about themselves and therefore their relationship to the world around them. This shift trickles throughout one's life and affects those around them.

I remember back to my dark days in high school—no self-esteem and isolated with depression. If only I had a teacher like you, things would have been different for me. What a gift you are and you are my Moomy. I am the luckiest girl in the world. I really feel incredibly blessed to have such an incredible relationship with my family. I love you so much. You are my best friend. I am so grateful for you and all that you give and do for me. Happy Mother's Day.
Love,
Tootsie

This made me so proud to be her mother. For all the things I didn't do, I was proud of giving her the gift of giving. I only wish that we had connected more when that lonely girl in high school was struggling. How could I support so many as a teacher, but somehow, someway, be unable to reach Lauren in high school? However, we were blessed with the love, admiration, and closeness over the last eight years. Again, Lauren's sobriety made this possible.

Lauren wanted to incorporate Rilke's eight principles into her coaching program, so here they are:

The Eight Principles of Rainer Maria Rilke:

1. Be patient with ourselves and others
2. Practice humility
3. Trust our intuition
4. Be personally responsible for our own inward discipline
5. Learn about ourselves through solitude
6. Concentrate through contemplation
7. Appreciate the beauty and good in nature and all things
8. Live the poetic spirit everyday

Lauren also sent me an email on Mother's Day on "The Divine Mother" and the characteristics that she stated only reflected on the traits that I saw in her. It was actually a mirror image, not only what she associated with me, but within herself. Lauren wrote, "The Divine Mother is an essential, nurturing, life-giving energy. She represents the power of beauty, the power of intuition, the power of creativity, the power of love."

It was easy for me to extend tenderness and joy to someone who, in spite of her struggles and demons, rose to many occasions with dignity and purity. This remarkable person was my daughter.

Lauren also thanked us for giving her the opportunity and encouragement to write. She felt our emotional support gave her the courage to develop a book and share her journey with others. She wanted to share these gifts. Her story has now become my story.

As mother and daughter, we clearly had our differences during her teen years. I wrote this letter March 2005, as I wanted her to move beyond what kept her back. It was inspired by Christiane Northrup's book on mother and daughter relationships.

Dear Lauren,

This is a letter that comes from my heart and soul. I love you and have always loved you. I may have fallen short at times. To the best of my ability, with the work of my body, the limits of my mind, and the strength of my soul, I have tried to give you love, as much of my time as possible in this hectic, hurried world. I have tried to give you fun and laughter. I have tried to give you safety and protection. My true intention has never been to hurt you or bring you any unnecessary pain. I have tried to be the best parent I could be with the tools given to me. I want you to know that for any times I have hurt you, disappointed you, or let you down, knowingly or unknowingly, I'm sorry. I am sorry for any shortcomings and the mistakes I made that caused you any pain. For this I ask your forgiveness.

Thank you for the pleasure and treasure you have given me. There has never been anything that you have done that has taken away my unconditional love for you. Always and now in my eyes, heart and soul, you are to me the most beautiful bud, the loveliest bloom and the most

perfect flower. I've loved you from the day you were born. I love you forever.
Love,
Moomy

On the other hand, as our adult relationship flourished, it was mandatory for a healthy relationship to see the good and bad, the love and hate, the black and white, without idealizing each other. Anyone who has loved anyone realistically will experience a rainbow of colors, moods and feelings that promote human nature. We usually stayed out of the dark waters of the struggling years and I wanted her to focus on the present, but it was imperative to acknowledge the negative, hidden feelings. I know I thought my mother was the queen of perfection, until I had some crucial therapy.

The clean mental, physical and holistic way of life was her way of developing her creative lifestyle. It gave her clarity. Staying present in time eased her fears and led her to a more pleasurable state of being. Through love and acceptance, her friends and sponsees developed their own sense of style, almost through osmosis and by tasting Lauren's world. She stood naked with many during their darkest hours, and from her own personal experiences, gave each young woman hope, faith, and courage to be their best.

Together, they created their own canvas like they were shopping for school supplies just prior to the first day of school. How would you like your world to be? What food, music, clothes, books, and colors would you like to set the tone? It was like a trip to self-discovery by getting in touch with the authentic self. Old habits, like numbing the body and mind, would dissipate, as new and long lasting ones would evolve.

Once again, Lauren would feel anxious, maybe in the middle of the night, often under tremendous stress. She would call me and I would hear a little girl, not unlike the five-year-old when she had the quicksand nightmares, and I would try to soothe her pain. Yes, I would throw her an invisible rope and we would chuckle under the covers, chatting coast to coast, like teenagers in high school. The fear would lift and the next day a new shift would transform from within her soul.

In the meantime, I wrote a letter that she kept, reminding herself that this would pass.

June, 2005
TO THE GIRL WITH THE KINDEST HEART:
Dear Lauren,
As I listened to you speak tonight, I heard a little girl that was in a lot of pain and rightfully so. Your chemicals are not quite right so the negative tapes set in. Okay, I do validate your feelings, but you are so off. Who else takes four trains to help others in Brooklyn at night? The angels are guiding you. This is part of your journey—not the pain and suffering, but the journey to dig into your soul and get through a horrible time. You are so lovely, so caring, and so strong and you don't even know it. Hang in there, baby. You sound better every day. We just haven't figured out the chemical part yet, but all is waiting for you. I promise you a good life. Lots of joy is on its way. You were meant to help others and give your gifts away. I honestly believe that there is no one like you. Really, who else goes to the Bel Air Hotel on her twenty-first birthday and meets another angel, only to fly off for a couple of hours and share from the soul. I believe in you. Always!
Love,
Mom

As I knew she would, Lauren became more vibrant and self-enlightened, after all of her struggles and disappointments. She finally figured out that there was light at the end of that damn tunnel and she would persevere like the trooper she was meant to be. Her father would proudly call her "a Zussman" and I would say, "Touché."

When Lauren had her Bat Mitzvah, we followed the customary tradition for the parents to read a letter during the service to give a message to their child. I told Lauren that we were proud of her accomplishments with sports and her academic achievement, but more importantly, I wanted her to know that we were proud of her for just being Lauren and that it was okay to be happy. I wanted her to welcome the joy field when it appeared and it was the first time that

I specifically told her to go for the gusto, a continuous theme that I enforced throughout her life. I looked her in the eye and said:

"Lauren, we are so proud of you for so many reasons. We want you to live each day to the fullest. Get the most from each hour, each day, and each age of your life. Be yourself, but be your best self. Dare to be different and to follow your own star. You are your own star, your own person; there is no doubt about that. Don't ever lose your spirit. Lauren, go for the gusto. Try and make the right choices. And if I can give you one message, it would be that it is okay to be happy. Don't be afraid to be happy and live in the moment."

I mentioned Rabbi Harold Kushner's philosophy on life for a grand finale at Lauren's Bat Mitzvah because he really said it best:

What Is Life About

"It is not about achieving beauty, writing great books, amassing great wealth or power. It is about loving and being loved. It is about savoring the beauty of moments that don't last: the sunsets, the leaves turning color, the rare moments of true human communication. It is about savoring them rather than missing out on them because we are so busy and they will not hold still until we get around to them. There is no answer, but there are answers—the little things that tend to get lost and trampled in when we have stopped searching. Instead, find ways of making each individual day a human experience."

☙

CHAPTER 11

Forty-Nine Days: The Release of an Angel

"Opportunity to find powers within ourselves comes when life seems most challenging."

Joseph Campbell

Lauren's eulogies were beautiful. I cherished what our Rabbi wrote. He so eloquently delivered his speech. It was a celebration of a life well-lived as he painted the canvas of Lauren's life span.

EULOGY FOR LAUREN ZUSSMAN

We walk today in the blackest darkness, assaulted by a nightmare from which we cannot awaken. A precious child has died, so unexpectedly— here one moment in all her inner loveliness and outer beauty, and then no more. Our minds reel; our hearts break; our souls are in anguish; our words cry out. They cry out to God.

This is not the natural order of things. We expect our children to outlive us. No parent should be asked to endure this terrible fate. What a light to her parents, who would have given anything to precede her. They will mourn for the rest of their lives, and how could it be otherwise?

Lauren Zussman's life was before her—love, family of her own, career. We can only imagine how many would have been beneficiaries of her giving, her compassion, her reaching out. Her dear sister Ashlie, her devoted family, her beloved Alex, her many and true friends, are bereft in their utter, unspeakable grief.

All the tomorrows that would have been, should have been. All the plans that would have been kept should have been kept. All the accomplishments that surely would have crowned her strivings, what now? Only memories of what was, what she did, who she became, what she meant. It is virtually impossible to believe that such a vibrant person as Lauren lies in that box.

It was a bittersweet moment when, at the house the other day, we watched Lauren's Bat Mitzvah video montage from half her lifetime ago. We saw her grow from baby to age 13: the home life, the celebrations, the vacations, the observances, the times of enjoyment and playfulness, photographs so sweet, so poignant.

Lauren was mesmerized by Italy and all things Italian: the people, the land, the sights, and the food. Italians and Jewish people have a great deal in common and I always say that an Italian is a Jewish person who drinks Chianti. I would speculate that part of what drew Lauren to Italy was the authenticity of the people, their depth and richness, their pride in who they are, thriving amid a colorful, bold, romantic culture.

Lauren died eight years to the day after the angel of death first drew near and almost claimed her. During those years, she was blessed with a second opportunity, a new lease on life, and she made the most of it. She became a person rich with sympathy and even empathy. As I listened to the tender reminiscences over the past days, I thought that Lauren was the epitome of Plato's advice: "Be kind to people, for everyone you meet is going through a struggle."

Lauren engaged with others of whatever age: sitting with adults undergoing chemotherapy, sponsoring people afflicted with addiction, inspiring disadvantaged young people, cautioning others about the *pitfalls of life's choices. She extended herself on behalf of people and they in turn gravitated to her.*

I met with Lauren but once. It was in my study that we talked years ago. She was emerging out of the most challenging period in her young life. Though we spoke only that time, the conversation is writ indelibly in my recollection. She expressed thoughts and feelings beyond her years, and I was impressed by her sense of spirituality. We established a bond that day and I was treated to a glimpse of her unique and special character.

Lauren died at her happiest, living life to its fullest, her days chock full of activity and pursuits, laughing in bloom, on the verge of entering her career as a life coach, on the threshold of new chapters in her book of life.

Now that book has been slammed shut, incomplete. So many pages are left blank that would rightly be filled with a chronicle of Lauren's passion for life and commitment to others.

Years ago, Lauren voiced a premonition that she would not live a long life. Over recent years, especially, Lauren made up for the threat of life's threatened end with heightened passion, striving for excellence and the pursuit of her vision.

I earlier mentioned Lauren's new lease on life. It is an apt expression, for we only lease life, we do not own it.

This is God's universe, not ours. It proceeds on his timetable, not ours. In God's infinite wisdom and from his eternal perspective, he deemed it time for Lauren's soul to return. Her spirit is now welcomed in heaven, into arms stronger than ours. May she rest in peace. May God keep her for all eternity. May memories of her genuine love and loyal friendship sustain us now and always.

In Christianity, Judaism and Buddhism, the belief is shared that we are here on earth for a given amount of time. We are only renting the earth. Regarding the philosophy of Buddhism, it takes forty-nine days for the spirit to go on to the next level, perhaps Heaven. I am not sure about that but I do believe that energy cannot be created or destroyed; therefore, our Lauren's soul is somewhere.

Lauren's friends and our close friends beautifully speak about the transformation of a girl to an incredible woman. Lauren had gained a tremendous amount of wisdom through the Twelve Steps and mastered them, only to lead others. She was one of the most requested speakers and spent weekends guiding young at-risk girls at yoga retreats. Compassion, loyalty, empathy, along with her power of intuition helped many. Lauren was an avid reader of psychology books as she applied principles to not only herself, but to others. Her girlfriends, and she had many, cherished her wisdom and companionship. Many came in from New York, San Francisco and Los Angeles to reflect their love and respect for their soul sister. If Lauren loved you, she loved you unconditionally and with great gratitude. She was quiet and humble with her wisdom, never intimidating others. The triumphs over her struggles became a teaching guide to others and that was her mission. She was a sage with deep insight.

Lauren helped a woman conquer her cancer and gave her comforting support. Renee wrote:

I experienced love and kindness with your daughter, Lauren. She sat next to me in group, would hold my hand and rub my neck the day before chemotherapy treatments. Lauren would try and relax me because I was so frightened. I trusted her healing hands and heart: her true love and concern for me. I would then lay my head on her shoulder and the fear would subside. Sometimes I would just weep, hoping that these treatments would end soon. She felt my pain and helped me so. You raised a loving angel, a real angel.

Renee was an older woman and although she was not as old as Grandma Janet, she reminded Lauren of her kind, loving Grandma. Lauren loved the wisdom of older people. She would ask them about their journey and what they had learned.

Michael Zussman is Lauren's close cousin and dear friend. Being a couple of months apart, they grew up together and at age 5, Michael asked his Rabbi if he could marry his cousin. Michael was the brother Lauren never had, and they could have passed for twins. The spiritual connection grew deep the last few years and they were always connecting by phone or visits. The eulogy was a presentation like no other, as Michael remembered the gifts of Lauren. Michael knew that in order to save herself, Lauren had to save others and she did it from the heart. Michael quoted J.D. Salinger's *Catcher in the Rye*, depicting the drive of Lauren's soul:

"I keep picturing all these little kids playing some game in this big field of rye and all. Thousands of little kids, and nobody's around—nobody big, I mean except [her]. And [she's] standing on the edge of some crazy cliff. What [she] had to do, [she] has to catch everybody if they start to go over the cliff—I mean if they're running and they don't look where they're going [she] has to come out from somewhere and catch them. That's all [she'd] do all day. [She'd] just be the catcher in the rye and all. I know it's crazy but that's the only thing [she'd] really like to be."

And then Michael, having a handsome, theatrical presence, continued with his own words, reflecting the true essence of Lauren. They shared their adventures and always discussed the complexities of love, work, and life. Michael gave one of the most insightful eulogies pegging Lauren at her best:

"She was elegant, kind, understanding, wise, and incredibly selfless. She was a Teacher, a Guide, a Friend, and in her own unique way, a gifted Healer. Lauren inhaled deeply from life and gracefully exhaled, breathing life back into the many people all around her, people who weren't quite sure if they could take another breath alone. Lauren dedicated her life to making sure that those people never felt alone again. You could always sense how much Lauren cared by how closely she listened, an innate ability which was, without a doubt, one of her most beautiful traits. You would speak and Lauren would be right across from you, looking at you in the eye, focused, composed, and always empathetic. She would take it all in and then after you'd finished getting it all out, she'd respond with wisdom—wisdom rarely found in any person. Above all else, Lauren was in love with her family—her immediate family in California and her extended family, all the souls she touched through her work, all the lives she changed through her love. Then I started to think about what Lauren would have wanted me to do with this time, what she would have wanted me to say. She would have asked me to help all the people who loved her find a way to cope. She would have asked me to say something that could in some way, to some degree, lessen the pain and the suffering we all currently feel and share with one another. So here is my best shot:

"I knew only one thing—which I have learned well by now: Love goes very far beyond the physical person of the beloved. It finds its deepest meaning in his spiritual being, his inner self. Whether or not she is actually present, whether or not she is still alive at all, ceases somehow to be of importance…nothing could touch the strength of our love, our thoughts, and the image of our beloved… Set us like a seal upon the heart, love is as strong as death."

Mans' Search for Meaning, Victor Frankl

As the tears flowed throughout the service, Lauren's love, Alex, stepped up to the podium, handsome as ever, with a quiet, regal presence. Alex and his entire family flew in for the funeral. We had never met his family before. This visit should have been for a wedding, not a funeral.

We were all drawn to his every word with conviction that he knew her best. Alex read the poem that Lauren had written to Alex just weeks before her passing when we were at Laguna Beach. Just days after their romantic, fairytale weekend, the love of Lauren's life, with sad and tired eyes, gave a moving dedication to their bond that will live on forever.

In His Arms

Sitting on the edge of the earth
Lost in the beauty of the ocean's deep blue seas
The waves dance and crash with passion and caress my soul
I am mesmerized by the glistening waves telling me secrets
The light illuminates the truth and I just know
The ocean breathes wisdom and promise
When I see the ocean I think of you and I know you are always
with me in my heart
In his arms, time escapes
In his arms, the jigsaw puzzle is completed
In his arms, the truth is clear

In his arms, it's the peace and stillness after the perfect storm
In his arms, I feel warmth of the brightest sunshine
In his arms, I know I am safe
In his arms, I am home at last

Love,
Lauren

The cause of death was the perfect storm of variables for Lauren to go into cardiac arrest, while jogging with Alex in Central Park, and Lauren actually died "In His Arms." A synchronicity exists that is unexplainable.

Two weeks later, Alex wrote the following eulogy in New York. Two hundred and fifty people attended a memorial for those who could not attend the LA funeral. We could not attend, as we were frozen in our pain, but a video of the service was soon sent to us.

"With Lauren, I was provided life's greatest blessings—to experience true love, pure and absolute. She beckoned my hesitant soul and expanded my heart with each passing day. Lauren's love of life was infectious. Though she was never able to win me over to the benefits of Stevia Extract, warm tap water, or macrobiotic organic rabbit food, I loved her all the more for her efforts. A gift of sobriety is my ability to look at the time we had with profound gratitude. I was able to stay present, speak from my heart, and love her with fierce abandon. Lauren was a very real person that overcame life's great challenges. Her capacity to love was matched only by her faith in God and herself. Loving Lauren, I felt closer to God and, laughing with her, I felt myself speaking his language. We spent her final hours absorbed in beauty and laughter. Her parting gaze was of streams of sunlight reflecting off water's gentle promise. I will now read a poem I wrote about her last day."

The sunlight cascaded off your face,
Eyes of promise and purpose,
Eyes of love.

Suddenly, holding you in my arms
Your trembling rib cage,
A bird's broken wing.

The heart, your greatest gift,
Was what you led with
And it sang of life.

It grew to fire, your heart,
and you returned home.

That sunlight, your first love,
mocked me with your passing
It illuminated a world dark
without my love.

And yet, this anguish lies not,
These tears depart freely
From a soul that holds you still.

It is after her funeral in Los Angeles. We have 150 people in our Newport Beach home. Friends, neighbors, and co-workers assemble throughout our house and joyous stories circulate as we celebrate the life of this extraordinary young woman.

One tall handsome young man, Scott, comes up to me to tell me his state of sobriety only comes from working with Lauren. Without her assistance, he wouldn't have committed to his Twelve Step program. Many cards, letters and e-mails continue to arrive stating the remarkable impact that Lauren had on all these people.

The New York memorial was on Friday the 13th. Lauren had a couple of dangerous close calls on many Friday the 13ths. When she was two, a sliding door fell on her head because it was not stationed on the runner. I was pregnant with Ashlie and David was at his office. Lauren had eighteen stitches and was lucky to not have any serious complications. Lauren also had a few pine nut allergy mishaps that brought her to the emergency room. Pine nut allergies or any allergies can close the throat and even cause death. Regardless of the date, her service with all those friends was an incredible dedication to a much loved soul.

We have three incidents when glass is shattered and we feel it had something to do with Lauren's spirit. When we are driving ten minutes away from the chapel, on the day of the funeral, the side glass window where David is sitting shatters into a million pieces. Ash and I are in the back seats and we first think that someone has shot at the car. Nothing hit the window, and we immediately think it is the strong energy of Lauren's spirit saying "I am here". The next day Ash finds two wine glasses in her dishwasher, shattered into pieces. Days later David and I quietly celebrate my birthday with one glass of wine that shatters in my hand for no apparent reason. Is someone wishing me a happy birthday? Some unknown person from New York sends me an e-mail stating not to fix a broken window, for the spirit will want to come in.

Ashlie sets up a memorial for Lauren online (Memory-of.com) and the loving comments and tributes come onto the web with great gratitude and dedication, nationally and internationally. Pictures of Lauren's friends and family are proudly displayed by her sister.

I start reading all the books on grieving the loss of a child. Many are sent to me, and some I buy. I also read about the five stages of grieving, something that I read in the past. I had a couple of miscarriages, one late in pregnancy, and I had to cope with loss. My mother, who was incredibly close with my family, died ten days after 9/11. We were all crazed over 9/11 and then my Mom died with no warning. However, she was nearly eighty-five years old, and although I was in shock and mourning her loss, the fact is, she had a full and happy life. Parents are not supposed to bury their children. I always thought I was lucky and yet, there was no logic to this death.

The only way I can get through the first painful weeks is to believe that perhaps it was her time. Maybe she was given eight years from her "Lake Havasu" nightmare to turn herself around, find the meaning to life, and leave this earth at her happiest. However, I would do anything to have her back: to hold her, to laugh with her, to exchange our spiritual words of wisdom.

David and I cry often, every day, and hold each other when the other one is weak. We have pictures everywhere of her smiling face. Particularly her latest ones reflect a healthy, vibrant shining star: our star, our flower, our sweet Lauren.

I got married on Memorial Day at age 26, only to leave behind my single life and enter a state of union. Our daughter died on Memorial Day at age 26, only to leave life and enter Heaven or an unexplained plane of another energy source.

We will never know, while on earth, the reason why she was taken at such an early age. But I must preserve her memory and state clearly that staying sober through growth and perseverance can be maintained by all, young and old. Lauren never wavered on her journey, even during the dark days. Every day became brighter for her, as she climbed her mountain and reached for the stars. Although I cannot do her justice with the profound impact that she would have had, I must try to somehow be her voice.

෧෨

CHAPTER 12

Mourning and Grieving:
Celebrating a Life Well-Lived

"Grief can be the garden of compassion."

Rumi

My chosen poem was read by a friend at the service, and it could not be topped by any other words. It said it all and from the bottom of my heart. The author is unknown.

The Cord
We are connected,
My child and I, by
An invisible cord
Not seen by the eye
It's not like the cord
That connects us 'til birth
This cord can't been seen

By any on Earth
The cord does its work
Right from the start
It binds us together
Attached to my heart
I know that it's there
Though no one can see
The invisible cord
From my child to me
The strength of this cord
Is hard to describe
It can't be destroyed
It can't be denied.
It's stronger than any cord
Man could create
It withstands the test
Can hold any weight
Though you're not here with me,
The cord is still there
But no one can see
It pulls at my heart
I am bruised…I am sore,
But this cord is my lifeline
As never before
I am thankful that God
Connects us this way
A mother and child
Death can't take it away!

Love,
Moomy

After a few weeks of grieving, I sat in the garden and wrote Lauren a letter as the hummingbirds gathered around the bird feeder. I spent most of the summer trying to hold on to myself and my family. Sitting very quietly with nature brought these profound feelings to the surface.

Dear Lauren,

Temporarily, there is no value to life when you lose a child. I am now on the outside, looking into other houses of life and laughter. I belong to a club that no one wants to join, nor should they. The ebb and flow of the realization of death, being so final, terrifies my soul. Shock waves continue, as a sense of denial weaves its way back and forth, to a false sense of security. The conveyor belt of confusion, anger, sadness, guilt and dread, continues on as a quiet death within me permeates.

The soothing music in the background, the burning candles, the comfort of your maroon shawl, surround the many sleepless nights of me grieving. Photographs and visual memories of your flesh, your energy, and your breathtaking smile appear in the corner of my mind, as the wick from the candle illuminates the dark room. As I sip my cup of vanilla chai tea, your favorite evening pleasure, I quietly wipe my tears, staring at the light, as memories drift in and out. From childhood woes, to witnessing a mature woman evolving through the disparity of life, I see an orange-red poppy in the wind, a calming sea connecting to a strong sunny light beam, a peaceful first snowfall on a mountain. It is your essence appearing, disguised as nature, as God, as a power that is unexplainable.

But then again, the pendulum swings to the other side. The quiet absence of your being, whether by phone or in person, leaves me empty everyday with endless sorrow. My amputated limbs leave my body with an empty shell. I fear that I will not feel life, as I have known it. The past is now a dream, as I have crossed over to the other side with you, my darling. And although I am still here on earth, I can never relive that lifeline between you and me, even though I know in my heart that the imaginary cord will always unite us.

Most days, I am swimming upstream, fearing that my drive to survive will wilt like a dried-out plant, or an overripe piece of fruit. As each sunrise and sunset creates distance of you leaving, I feel my soul hibernating, hoping that with time, the pure essence of your existence will take center stage in my mind again. The pain of reality has offset your thriving life, and must be remembered as God wanted it to be.

From the beaches to the mountains, I promise to honor you through nature. You have taught me, sweet Lauren, to have an open heart, unconditional love and to be of service to others in need.

I will always carry your voice, your passions, your incredible love for your friends and your family, for you just got it, the true meaning of life, before most of us ever did. I will carry you on my shoulder for a lifetime.

When I see the purity of a dove, the snow white orchid, or the iridescent moon, I will smile, knowing that your memory will live on through all of our hearts. We are simply better people because your human spirit has taught us so much about life.

Even though my broken heart has lost its desire to sing and dance, I will never let the memory of your spirit die, for you are one in a million, with an inner life that will live on forever.
Love,
Moomy

It has been several months since Lauren's passing and time has given us periods of normalcy, although, as my husband has said, "we have to create a new normal." I must have the courage to go on, not only for myself, but more importantly, for my husband and for Ashlie. A sibling has many phases to go through dealing with the loss of a sister. We are so proud of how she has honored her sister with an incredible web site and all that she has accomplished during this difficult time. We all wear a silver chain bracelet with "COURAGE" engraved on one side and "LAUREN 08" on the other side. Lauren's courage inspires us, as she would so not want us to suffer.

My memories of her coming home, to our bed parties with her favorite foods, to reading magazines and studying fashion together, remind me of a girl stirring with delight. Tea parties and back scratching went along with watching old Richard Gere movies (especially *Pretty Woman, Autumn in New York*, and *An Officer and a Gentleman*) or *Grey's Anatomy*, laughing once again, at *Romy and Michele*, or commenting on each young celebrity and their dramatic life. Eating salmon with veggies drenched in olive oil, or eating endless bowls of my homemade soups—these memories put a smile on my face every time. Listening to her favorite singer, Ray La Montagne, stirs our souls.

Her Bohemian style of dress, similar to a French savvy woman, had a unique style of its own, with wrapped-around colorful scarves and gypsy-style skirts, yet I envision her donning a t-shirt, jeans and boots. Lauren walked with poise and dignity, even when she had her long, flowing, chestnut hair in a ponytail under a cap hat, wearing sweats.

Our endless conversations about the latest spiritual book, or a profound weekend movie, were moving to both of us. Sometimes a report on a weekend of lectures from well-known sages contributed to her bank of knowledge. I will miss the intimate dance of meaningful conversations that comes from trust and love. I will miss the give and take of sharing our human sides when we would often hide from the real world.

Coming home to the sun and water only reminded her of how much she missed Southern California. I watched her jump the waves and bask in the sunshine. It would be only a matter of time before she would return to the West Coast. It was home.

We would speak fondly of Grandma Janet and our family dog, Muffy, both deceased, and suddenly nostalgic smiles would appear on our faces. I hope that she is with them, today.

We all reminisced about the endearing convertible ride home from the airport, each time Lauren flew home from New York. Along with her daddy, holding hands with the wind blowing through her hair, they listened to Bill Medley's "This Will Be the Last Time." This was the essence of true living.

I think about all the adventures she had with her sister. Ash keeps telling us the mischievous stories, harmless but sneaky, as their endless love for each other continues forever.

While visiting from New York, just months before her passing, I remember Lauren requesting a Labor Day party with all of our friends. When Lauren came to visit, she would often only want to be with us, but this time she wanted to celebrate with our friends. A gathering of twenty joyfully assembled though out the house. Her dear cousin Michael and best friends, Amanda and Jessica, also joined the party. I watched Lauren interact with the company, as she gracefully flowed from person to person, like a butterfly ready to land on a scented flower.

Lauren leaned in to listen intently, touched your arm with empathy, and asked questions with her warm, chocolate-brown eyes, always wanting to know about your state of being. "What life challenges have you had to overcome? What joy have you found along the way?"

Lauren knew that life lessons only make you stronger. She learned to finally embrace the lightness with the darkness, the calm with the rocky waters, and the unknown with the certainties of life.

She also had a way of bringing the goodness out in people. When she would respond with words of wisdom, spoken in a soft, soothing voice, the concept of unconditional love would set in their souls, being the main ingredient of the conversation. The mirror image of love and self-acceptance played off between them, like the sun's reflection off a calm, blue lake. It became a contagious state of being.

I hope that Lauren is with nature, for she so loved the fragrant flowers, billowing trees, scented gardens and flowing lakes. I also hope that they have coffee houses and bookstores in Heaven.

But most of all, I think being of service to others gave her the greatest joy and perhaps after helping many, she spread her wings to help a new breed of needy souls, in another land, or on another plane. Why else would her life have ended so abruptly?

Many times, growing up, we made visual memories by closing our eyes during special times, like when we got a kitten, or moved into a new house. The wonder of the remarkable memories were cherished throughout the years. I now hang on to our memories, daily, sometimes crying, sometimes smiling. My soul is depleted, my spirit is broken, but I hang on to that cord, that rope, knowing that I will never relinquish it completely.

Lauren loved fairies and we have a statue of a fairy reading a book that looks a lot like her, sitting in our garden, and of course we now have the bird feeder, with hummingbirds flying to it daily, as we greet Lauren's spirit.

We have such bittersweet memories, ebbing and flowing, as we had to stay quiet during this time. David and I shared a common, intimate experience of being in an indescribable state of being. It was very surreal. Silence is something so foreign to both of us. We tried desperately to absorb the shock, the emptiness, the sadness, that overcame our bodies daily. At the time, we had no relief. Moment by moment, hour by hour, this nightmare embedded around us as we tried to get through the days.

Our friends and family have been phenomenal, and I don't think we could have started the healing process without them. It is only recently that we started to accept social invitations, but mostly, we like to stay close to home. One day could be a good day, only to be saddened with our loss the next day. There is no prescription to grieving.

Sweet Alex has visited with us a few times during the last several months. There is no question in our minds that Lauren and Alex were meant to be together. I did not meet Alex until after Lauren's passing. Lauren couldn't wait for the family reunion and for us to meet him. I knew he had to be a winner.

I wrote a letter to Alex, not so long ago.

Dear Alex,

You have been on my mind the last few days. We are all doing the best we can, given the tools we have, to get through our darkest hours and days. There is no formula or advice that one can give to deal with this tragedy, as we all heal in our own time. But I do believe in hope for the future, faith in God, and courage not only for my family, but for all of us to move beyond this pain and suffering. Our sweet Lauren would want this.

I hope we learn something from all of this. I am not sure what that may be, but our journey has not ended; therefore, we do not know what lies ahead.

As I have spoken to you about your future years to come, I see a man evolving to a new awakening. Grieving is a lot to process, but I promise you, life will get better. David and I care deeply about you and your well-being.

I know this year will shift to a new direction, upon moving and relocating to a new environment. A new beginning awaits you. In the meantime, I hope you find simple pleasures during your down time from work.

Once again, we are always here for you, as Lauren too, smiles from above on all of us.
Fondly,
Lynda

January 31, was Lauren's birthday. David and I went to a soup kitchen to serve food. This was not only to honor our daughter, but it would be something Lauren would have done. It also helped us get through the day. Our girl would have been twenty-eight years old.

I try to be with nature every day, reaching out for a glimpse of Lauren's spirit. The abstract, frosty clouds after a heavy rainfall, a full moon with radiating beams, or a picturesque view of the ocean touch my soul, with Lauren's arms wrapped around me.

Upon waking every morning, I pray that the day will have some meaning, some value, to carry on, or to make this a better place to live.

At the conclusion of the funeral, a poem was read about our loved ones being with us, not physically, but spiritually. With the intensity of Lauren's energy, I know that she surrounds all of us but in a different form.

I Am Not There

Do not stand at my grave and weep,
I am not there. I do not sleep.
I am a thousand winds that blow,
I am the snow on the mountain's rim,
I am the laughter in children's eyes,
I am the sand at the water's edge,
I am the sunlight on ripened grain,
I am the gentle Autumn rain,
When you awaken in the morning's hush,
I am the swift uplifting rush of quiet birds in circled flight,
I am the star that shines at night,
Do not stand at my grave and cry,
I am not there, I did not die.

Author Unknown

Recently I watched the Hallmark movie *When Love Is Not Enough – The Mary Wilson Story* from my bed in my bedroom. Towards the end of the movie, depicting the struggle and victory of Bill and Mary

Wilson, battling alcoholism and coping with an alcoholic husband, I was moved and crying from the impact of the message—people helping people and staying sober. I thought about how Lauren would have loved the movie and as I felt her presence, my eyes drifted to the wood floor, only to be shocked to see a little, live gray-haired rabbit. I was speechless and called for David to see this incredible, helpless bunny eyeballing me with an intense glare. How did this animal get in the house, up to the second floor, while I was engrossed in this movie? If she came through the doggie door, how did this bunny pass by our two dogs without being noticed? This will always be an enigma to us. As crazy as this sounds, could this somehow be the spirit of Lauren?

Just as eerie as this seems to be, we are haunted by a light that mysteriously lit up as we were sleeping. David and I went to our storage garage to sort through Lauren's belongings. We had a very difficult time that day and I had to chill out that night and crash. In Lauren's turquoise shawl, I lit candles, wrote in my journal and played Ray La Montagne songs. I went to bed that night tired, worn out and grieving. With David next to me, the light on my make-up table turned on. I woke David and pointed this out to him. I got up and turned it off, only for it to go back on within minutes. It spooked David the second time it turned on. He has always been a non-believer in the spiritual world. When it came on a third time, he finally said to me, "Stop channeling her, this is giving me the willies."

I will always be open to signs of Lauren's energy source. That is all I can say. Without apologies, I accept whatever taps into my soul without over-analyzing the situation. The mystery of life happens every day in the universe.

As I would have envisioned a future life for Lauren, I could only wish for her a good life—a life well-lived.

Eight Wishes for My Daughter:
1. To be physically and mentally healthy
2. To love your work in life
3. To find a great partner to love, honor and cherish
4. To reach many with your exceptional gifts
5. To take any sorrow, pain, disappointments and use that experience to help others

6. To appreciate your daily state of being with gratitude
7. To maybe have children and pass your gifts to them
8. To be one with God and the Universe

As I wrote this, I realized that Lauren had achieved almost all of the above, except number 7. However, she will touch the children at The Orangewood Children's Home in Santa Ana, California as contributions and volunteers continue to flourish in her honor. Again Toots, your fairy dust is here making a difference.

In the meantime, sweet daughter, we need you to *THROW US THE ROPE.*

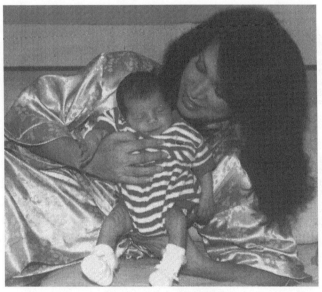

Valentine's Day 1982

❧

EPILOGUE

I observed Lauren persevering through each year of sobriety as she handled her pain, despair, loneliness, sorrow and anger. Each success took her to a new level. Life never stands still. The challenges of life are endless and we are all put to the test daily. Perhaps we need to stay in the moment, learn from our experiences, and become wiser the next time we experience loss and disappointment. Hope, faith, and courage can weather almost any storm. I am now trying to remember this daily. I have learned a lot from Lauren.

I told Lauren that her depression, which became less and less as she empowered herself with magnificent tools, was just a finger of her personality. With all her gifts, her delightful traits, her humorous, giving soul, how could she let a label take center stage? And best of all, her human kindness was always throwing someone the rope, sometimes to a sponsee, to a friend or helping out at a soup kitchen. We all need to do just that.

I try to have small, simple pleasures while I am trying to heal. I hope to help young, struggling women in the future—a center to heal and thrive would be my dream. Art and music therapy would be an added element, along with caring, helpful people. We are all here to help and support each other. I hope Lauren's voice will reach millions.

I know now, more than ever, that family and close friends are everything. Absolutely everything! Everything else is secondary. Hopefully, someway, somehow, someday, I hope "The Rollies" will all be together, eating, playing, and laughing together aboard the cuckoo train. I so miss those days and at the same time I am so grateful to have had my family in tack for thirty years. I am hoping that the pain of Lauren leaving, at such a young age, transfers to the light of her being. Lauren was a joy to all of us and I know her spirit will live on within all of us.

ACKNOWLEDGEMENTS

I want to thank Bill W. and his Angels for contributing to the sober success of millions.

I want to thank my family for always being there in times of our darkest hours: Judy and Harold Ticktin, Roger and Pat Charley Brown, Marc and Tami Zussman and family. Michael Zussman, you are the brother Lauren never had and the best cousin.

Our dear friends were right there with love, hugs and support: Rabbi Mark Miller, Judy Geller, Steve Verchick, Tana Sherwood, Fran Cey, Alex and Rick Bullard, Patti and Jerry Grice, and Trudy and Bruce Fagel. Thank you to my readers: Viki Iffland, Emily Dwass, Debra Cross, Mary Consul and Amy Rothermund. Thank you for continuous support from Judi Lampe, Kathy Davis, Denise Snyder and Penny Meisler: All of you are my sisters. Thank you Michael Levin for your support and advice.

I want to thank the doctors that have helped us: Dr. Marlene Laping, Dr. Jeffrey Bruss, Dr. Edward Kaufman, Dr. Lawrence Allison, and Dr. Gregory Katz. A special thanks to Dr. Frank Garrido at Lenox Hills Hospital and his staff.

And to Lauren's sisters and brothers from AA: You have become members of our family, as Lauren is smiling down on all of us: Gina M., Kate C., Marta K., Gabby B., Gabby R. Robyn S., Donna S., Dr. Donna,

Christian, Billie B., Jessica, and Carolina. Thank you for the loving eulogies and childhood friendships: Jessica, Lindsay and Amanda.

I am also so very grateful for the WW girls, Lori Chozen, Kelli Norris and Lorraine Leavitt, for our lunches and friendship. Thanks for getting me up and out and always being there through the laughter and tears.

Thank you, dear Alex, for loving our girl. You made her so happy and you will always be part of our extended family.

Many thanks to my Ash Mash, Bunky girl. I am so proud of you for your incredible strength, wisdom, love and support. You're everything a parent would want in a daughter and so much more.

Lastly, I want to thank my beloved husband, David, as we stand side by side, going through this journey, while we try to make a new normal.

∽

Made in the USA
Lexington, KY
21 November 2011